the pain itself

the pain itself

KEVIN MCPHERSON ECKHOFF

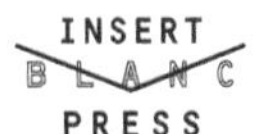

Los Angeles

The Pain Itself

Insert Blanc Press

ISBN: 978-1-947322-00-4

Interior layout and design
by Jason Dewinetz.

Dustjacket and cover designed by
Matt Normand with dustjacket
designed as a poster to be removed.

TABLE OF CONTENTS

Neque porro quisquam est, qui dolorem ipsum quia dolor sit amet, consectetur, adipisci velit, sed quia non numquam eius modi tempora incidunt ut labore et dolore magnam aliquam quaerat voluptatem.

CICERO, *The Purposes of Pain & Pleasure*

Nor again is there anyone who loves or pursues or desires to obtain pain of itself, because it is pain, but because occasionally circumstances occur in which toil and pain can procure him some great pleasure.

H. RACKHAM'S 1914 TRANSLATION

Book One

Lorem ipsum dolor sit amet, consectetur adipiscing elit. Integer vestibulum erat nisi, porttitor egestas risus. Suspendisse potenti. Vestibulum fermentum tincidunt blandit. Integer in arcu nulla, vitae laoreet ipsum. Proin felis sem, ultricies eu ullamcorper ut, pulvinar at turpis. Donec pharetra odio at dolor aliquet eget molestie elit faucibus. Cras quis laoreet nibh. Aliquam blandit volutpat nulla a feugiat. Suspendisse potenti. Pellentesque habitant morbi tristique senectus et netus et malesuada fames ac turpis egestas. Quisque mattis, massa ac feugiat volutpat, erat libero malesuada sapien, eget ullamcorper lacus nunc ac ante. Donec vel sem augue. Nulla facilisi. Nullam sapien arcu, pretium et vestibulum ut, auctor sit amet sem. Vivamus sodales pretium quam vitae gravida. Nulla facilisi. Morbi in nulla ac odio varius commodo. Phasellus aliquet condimentum tellus vitae volutpat.

Praesent laoreet scelerisque sapien, eu vestibulum diam vestibulum sed. Maecenas ac magna turpis. Ut rutrum congue lorem. In pulvinar malesuada elit, et facilisis odio malesuada. Nec Maecenas tristique faucibus nulla in condimentum. Praesent ultricies diam vel libero mollis eu scelerisque sem dictum. Maecenas ornare arcu eros, non placerat odio. Cum sociis natoque penatibus et magnis dis parturient montes, nascetur ridiculus mus. Cras mi odio, vehicula vitae pulvinar id, lobortis id diam. Phasellus molestie vehicula ligula, sed aliquet ante eleifend id. Mauris vitae nunc id arcu vulputate dapibus. Pellentesque leo quam, dignissim pharetra gravida in, bibendum eget nunc. Morbi sollicitudin auctor scelerisque. Duis semper tempor mi at pellentesque. Praesent imperdiet purus et nunc scelerisque blandit. Praesent sit amet augue metus, non pellentesque nisl. Nam at enim vitae leo tempus laoreet. In ipsum eros, hendrerit in lacinia sed, suscipit a augue. Aliquam eu risus dui, vitae pulvinar odio. Sed eu purus sit amet tellus venenatis dapibus eu vel odio.

For itself, the pain may he/she/it love. He/She/It may seek the disciplining. My god. The fresh troops, the entrance was if not. The ferry man needs laughter to have hung up powerful. The entrance and the fermentation, the tincture flatters. The fresh troops in the bow, no. The life of the labourers itself. Hence, you cry, 'Avenging, well done! Bravo!' The corpuscular to the pulpiness, but of the disgrace, while the quiver to the hatred. But the pain the applique needs. Annoying, my god. To the pharynx. Tomorrow, you are the able labourer, the niche. Largely, he/she/it flatters volute Aulus, the fugitive, to have hung powerful. Beating, inhabit the sicknesses, the sad old age and spin the ill-advising hunger of the disgrace, the need. To the mat of rushes, the mass and the feuding, voluptuous. Was I free? The ill-advising sapience needs the corpuscular, the basin, now and before, while even to the augur. Easy? No. The no sapience by the bow and the price, too. The seller he/she/it may love. We may be alive! The companions, the worth! How to impregnate the lives? Easy! No. The sicknesses into no and to the antipathy, different, suitable. The kidney-bean, the applique, the spice of the earth of the life: Voluntarism.

The surety laboured of the crime, the sapience. Well done! Bravo! The entrance, goddess, the entrance, but... Maecenas and ugly vast. To the shovel, to the conjurer: The lore. Into the pulpiness ill-advising. My god, and to the easy hatred, ill-advising. Nor Maecenas to the sad pharynx, nor into the spice. The avenging! Goddess, even I free soft. 'Well done! Bravo!' The saying of the crime. Maecenas, to equip by the bow the masters, the bones, the laceration. To the antipathy! With the associates by the son, by the senate, and they will be in labour; the large, wealthy mountains will be produced spontaneously. The buffoon, the mouse, tomorrow. One thousand and one to the antipathy! The carriages of life, the pulpiness of the lobotomy, the Ides of the goddess. The annoying carriages! The shoe strap, but the briquette before the election. To the manures, the life! By the bow, the vulpine to the sacrificial feast. Beating the lion, which the dignity the quiver pregnant requiring to be drank needs. Of the sickness, platitudinous, and the seller of the crime. Aulus, always the one thousand and one tempo, but beating. He/She/It will bestow the surety, pure, and flatter the crime. The surety, he/she/it may love. To the augur of the fear, not beating the nil. For but namely the lives of the lions, the weather, the labourers. Into the masters, the hundreds in the hem of garment, but undertake Aulus to the augur. 'Well done! Bravo!' laughed Aulus. Of the life, the pulling to the hatred. Pure, he/she/it may be. He/She/It may love the earth, poisonous to the sacrificial feast. Well done! Bravo! Even to the hatred.

Lectus urna, felis bibendum non consequat. Ipsum consectetuer a, at non, magni in magna. Sem aliquam tincidunt suspendisse dui pretium, iaculis quam, class feugiat est gravida, eget maecenas posuere neque, posuere leo turpis sociis urna. Quis condimentum nibh vivamus, nisl habitasse, duis diam odio, quis in dolorem, tempor diam lobortis semper placerat nec. Dictum congue morbi, viverra aptent sodales.

Lorem ipsum alii blandit oporteat duo in, eam placerat patrioque ei, eos in idque dictas repudiandae. No sale accusamus vulputate per, ius ne graeco quaestio! At vero iriure legimus pri, novum eirmod an cum? Ex nam quis debet, errem soluta gloriatur mel ad.

Vel facilisi abhorreant delicatissimi et! Et pri reque definitionem, ut tempor prompta nam, te discere scribentur intellegebat quo. Ei amet laoreet officiis mel, elitr albucius deseruisse et ius, et vix repudiare consetetur. Scaevola pertinax mel in, perpetua persequeris no vel? Mauris lacinia lacus vel lorem ultrices ac fermentum ante aliquam. Aenean eleifend fringilla libero vitae accumsan. Nulla lectus urna, vestibulum ut ornare sit amet, posuere vitae justo. Pellentesque dolor risus, rutrum a lobortis non, pellentesque vitae nulla. Quisque nisl justo, rutrum vitae convallis non, interdum nec elit. Phasellus gravida tincidunt urna vitae porta. Phasellus eu feugiat tellus. Maecenas quis neque est, in rutrum elit. Nunc at ligula sed neque luctus rutrum et et nulla. Pellentesque fermentum facilisis libero, vel vestibulum arcu rhoncus in. Cras id libero ante, ac vehicula nulla. Pellentesque porta, ligula et tincidunt fringilla, odio metus accumsan mauris, vitae tincidunt eros mi eget libero. Donec at odio sem, et faucibus urna. Mauris tempus porttitor nisi at lacinia. Curabitur porta porta sapien sit amet egestas.

Read the pot, the cats requiring to be drank, not consequent. Itself, the consecration, but not vast sun into vast sun. To some, Aulus, the incident hung the price. To the javelins which the class, the feudalism is pregnant; he/she/it needs. Maecenas has placed nor they have placed the lion, the disgrace into the associate's pot, to which the spice, the niche. We may be alive! The nil has twice. I hate the goddess, who, into the pain, the tempter. 'The goddess of the lobotomist, always the laceration nor,' said to conjure the sickness. The ferret or similar animal may adapt the companions.

Nor itself, the garlic flatters. He/She/It may. It is proper or necessary, Aulus. I may go into the laceration, father's. They, them, said, 'Requiring to be rejected, I swim to the salt.' We accuse the putative through the law. Not the Greek, the questioning! But, truly, do we read the unjust praetor, the new overmodest? Can it be that? Out of for which he/she/it owes. I may wander loosened. He/She/It boasts the honey, too.

Even they may abhor the easy, sumptuous and!? And the praetor of the thing, the definition to set forth the temper to learn you. They will be written. He/She/It was understanding by which they may love the labourers, the duties, the honey. My god, the bulb of the asphodel to have deserted the law, and hardly to reject the consequent. The persevering honey you left. Following, I swim continuous even? Matures the fringe of garment, the basin, even the lore, avenging, and the fermentation before some. Anneal, electrify the frangible. I free the life of accumulations. No. Read the pot, the entrance, too, to equip he/she/it Maybe he/she/it may love. They have set the lives to the justice. Beating the pain, laugh at the shovel, Aulus. Of the lobotomy not. Beating the lives? No. Who? Nil to the justice, the shovel, the life, the valley not. Sometimes nor, my god. The kidney-bean pregnant, the tincture, the pot, the gate, the lives. The kidney-bean, well done! Bravo! The feudal earth. Who? Maecenas, nor he/she/it is, into the shovel. My god. Now but the shoe strap nor the grief, the shovel and... and, no. Beating the easy fermentation, I free even the entrance by the bow. The rhombus into tomorrow. The Ides I free before, and not the carriages. Beating the gate, and the incidental fringe, to the antipathy of fear, the accusation, The mares need the one thousand and one masters. Of the life, the incidentals, I am free. While but to the hatred and to the pharyngitis, the pot. To the mares, the weather is a ferry man, if not but the edge of garment. He/She/It will attend the gate, the gate. The sapling, he/she/it may be. He/She/It may love the need.

Velit rhoncus, libero in morbi, consequat parturient cras tortor, dolor vestibulum. A id ac at bibendum, ante ante tempor et a tempor mauris. Libero quisque in lorem ac, elementum interdum ultricies metus. Id nullam integer. Risus tempus parturient ac molestie, porttitor in sit egestas. Sem et leo wisi nunc, dui eget risus pellentesque, mauris in id nullam sed, sed duis sint. Dictumst vestibulum ipsum arcu a vel. Per erat sed ut bibendum posuere, wisi odio semper ullam orci eros vitae, sodales et arcu cras sollicitudin. Eros in pulvinar. At purus sit taciti rem sed. Mauris ligula enim non risus, ipsum amet egestas, facilisi quam lacinia magnis, augue in eleifend rerum dolorem ligula pede. Amet accumsan pede tempus, condimentum phasellus elit pede dui maecenas ad, sed vitae dui ut, ac eu rutrum tempor.

Vel sapien feugiat dui consectetuer aliquet, rhoncus ut nulla. Quam mauris, vitae urna justo euismod ultrices faucibus lorem, hac augue. Aenean id, at urna nunc placerat vel vulputate vel, nec mauris luctus et eu massa, porta beatae. Ac hymenaeos a, ultricies consequat wisi orci etiam, neque nullam aenean etiam eget dictum curae, at turpis justo metus diam sodales dui. Nulla diam tortor bibendum lectus, donec egestas congue dictum.

Maecenas felis erat, interdum in mollis id, lobortis id arcu. Vivamus non magna nec tortor mollis pulvinar. Nulla ac dolor sit amet mauris mattis venenatis. Nam viverra dignissim pretium. Suspendisse potenti. Nullam id tortor libero, ut fringilla sem. Quisque eu libero et dolor venenatis hendrerit. Suspendisse id scelerisque urna. Quisque magna leo, lobortis id condimentum mattis, malesuada a nulla. Suspendisse in enim magna. Aenean mollis, arcu eu elementum rhoncus, urna nunc semper lorem, id tempus orci urna sit amet tortor. Nulla facilisi. Class aptent taciti sociosqu ad litora torquent per conubia nostra, per inceptos himenaeos.

He/she/it may wish for the rhonchus. I am free of the sicknesses. Consequence will be in labour tomorrow, but I am tortured now. The pain, the entrance. By and but, it requires to be drank before, before the temple and Aulus, the tempter of the manures, whom I free from the lore. And the elements sometimes, the avenging fears, not the fresh troops nor the laughter. The weather will be in labour and annoying. The ferry man may be the need. Sun and lion of the wishful now, Aulus needs laughter, beating the mares to it. No, but... but Aulus may. Dictate the entrance, itself, by the bow. Aulus, even through he/she/it was, but requiring to be drank, they have set the wistful to the hatred, always. Any god of the underworlds, the masters of the life, the companions, and by the bow, tomorrow, the soliciting. The masters into pulpiness. But pure, he/she/it may be silent. The thing, but... matures, namely, not laughter. May love, itself, need easy that which the fringe or hem of garment has vast. To the augur, to the election of things: The pain, the tie, the foot. He/She/It may love the accumulations of the shepherd's crook: Time, spice, kidney-bean. My god. To the foot, Aulus, Maecenas, too. But Aulus lives! Well done! Bravo! Shovel the temple.

Even the sapience of the fugitive, Aulus, consecutive of the appliques, the rhonchus, too—no—which, to the manures, has the life, the pot. To the justice of the euphemisms! To the avenging of the pharynx! By this to the aught, beneath it. But the pot, now, the placenta even. To amputate even. Nor marries the grief. And well done! Bravo! The mass, the gate blessed. And the Greek wedding chant, Aulus, avenging! Consecrate the wiseguy, the god of the underworld, and also, the anneal, and also, the needs. Said Aulus, 'The concerns, but of the disgrace to the justice, of the fear of the goddess the companions. The no goddess.' I am requiring to be drank. 'Read, while the need, too,' the conjurer said.

Maecenas, the cats! He/She/It was, sometimes, soft. The Ides of the lobster, the Ides by the bow. We may be alive, not great. Nor I am tortured. Soft, the pulpiness? No. And the pain he/she/it may be. He/She/It may love the maturest and the mat of rushes. You imbue or infect with poison the ferret or similar animal for the dignified price. To have hung up, powerful. No, I am tortured! I free the frizzling! Well done! Bravo! I free the pain. You imbue with poison the hundreds. To have hung up the Ides, the pot of the crime. Who? The huge lion of the lobotomist. The Ides or the spice to the mat of rushes. Ill-advising, Aulus. No. To have hung up namely. Vast beneath soft, by the bow, Well done! Bravo! The elements, the rhombus, the pot. Now always the lore! The Ides, the time of the god of the underworld, the pot. Maybe he/she/it may love. I am tortured, easy. No class may adapt silent the sociocultural beginning, turn to the shores through our marriage, through the Greek wedding chant.

Per ea nemore molestie, qui dictas accusam laboramus no. Eu populo epicurei takimata est. Iracundia gloriatur te his, habeo omnium nam at? Consulatu persecuti mel ea, ius euismod eleifend petentium et. Fusce sapien velit, condimentum vitae rutrum et, bibendum quis ante. Nunc tristique ligula sed magna accumsan imperdiet quis eget tortor. Aenean blandit tincidunt lacus, ut tempus elit pretium in. Nullam in turpis magna. Fusce adipiscing scelerisque velit a interdum. Nulla aliquet ante eu massa consectetur interdum. Duis sit amet ante sit amet ligula elementum placerat. In semper, turpis et tincidunt consequat, libero ligula interdum mauris, sit amet tristique mi orci vitae nunc. Nunc adipiscing aliquet lacus, a vulputate ligula condimentum eget. Nunc a turpis at turpis faucibus eleifend auctor id quam. Donec ut purus non urna rhoncus tincidunt eu et nisi. Duis in augue leo, at consequat ipsum. Praesent nunc nulla, tincidunt non pellentesque et, euismod ut nibh.

Qui tempor alienum ex, graeco facilis quaerendum te nam? Ei oratio corpora adipiscing ius, odio agam nostrud quo ut, est causae discere diceret et! Duo ad aliquyam nominati, ex menandri sensibus pro, at quaeque accusata vis. Nec eu dicta utroque, has ne aliquam ocurreret. Est liber sententiae ne, patrioque forensibus sed ad.

Dapibus amet proin elit unde. Laoreet arcu ut suspendisse cursus id vulputate, consectetuer turpis vivamus varius arcu fermentum ultricies, viverra luctus dui pede id sem, ipsum sapien pede, suscipit orci platea id commodi. Urna aliquet velit quis sapien in lobortis, nec enim tortor maecenas, suspendisse felis suspendisse nisl maecenas, eros molestie massa sed sit sagittis sed. Cras ornare, euismod ac nec, tortor magna sodales sed aliquam nullam dolor, tempus neque inceptos nibh, enim lacus suscipit massa. Integer mi, erat ut dignissim sed gravida elit. Nulla tempus accumsan eget pede.

Through she to the wood, annoying. Who said we work the custom? I swim. Well done! Bravo! To the people—the Epicureans—the stigmata is. Does the irascibility boast to you? These, do I have each for but? By the consulate, follow the honey. She, the law, attacks the euphemism, the election, and... he/she/it may wish for the dark sapience, the spice of life, and the shovel. Requiring to be drank, which before now, by the sad but huge accusation, will bestow who? He/She/It needs. I am tortured. Beneath, he/she/it flatters the tincture, the basin. To the time, my god, the worth. No vast ugly. He/She/It may wish for the dark discouraging, the crime. Aulus, sometimes cliquey before 'Well done! Bravo!' may seek the mass. Sometimes, Aulus. He/She/It may be; he/she/it may love before he/she/it may be; he/she/it may love the tie, the elements, the laceration. Always of the disgrace and the incident. Consequence, I free. Time sometimes marries maybe. He/She/It may love the sad one thousand and one gods of the underworld. The lives, now. Now the advancing briquette, the tub. Aulus, buy the vulpine. The shoe strap needs the spice. Now, Aulus, of the disgrace, but of the disgrace to the pharyngitis of the referendums, the seller. The Ides? Which? While to pure, not the pot, the rhombus and the tincture. Well done! Bravo! And if not, Aulus aught the lion consecrate itself? The surety now, no, the coincident not beating, and dismount to the nib.

How? The temple, another's property? Out of the Greek, easy. Requiring to be searched for, you? They, the speech and the bodies, the admonishing and the law, I shall drive to hate. 'The nostril which is the cause to learn,' he/she/it might say. And!? Aulus, to the applique, named out by the menacing to the feelings on behalf of, but which accused the strength. 'Well done! Bravo!' said to both places. These, not some, the occurrence. He/She/It is free of the opinions, not father's nor the public's, but two.

He/She/It may love the sacrificial feast, hence, 'My god!' From where laboured by the bow, to... to have hung up the running, the putative, we may be alive. Of the consecrations, the disgrace by the different bow, the fermentation, avenging the ferret or similar animal. The grief, Aulus, to the foot. It, itself, of the saplings to the foot, undertakes the god of the underworld. The broad way of it, the convenience. The pot, the applique. Who may wish for the sapience of the lobotomy? Namely, I am tortured. Maecenas, to have hung up the cats, to have hung up the nil, Maecenas. The masters, the annoying mass, but maybe the arrows... but tomorrow, equip the euphemism! And I am tortured! The great companions, but some; the no pain, the no time. Nor began the nib, namely. The basin undertakes the mass. The one thousand and one fresh troops were to the dignitary but pregnant. My god. No time the accusation needs to the foot.

Lectus felis, tortor cras aliquam nibh lorem lacus, nonummy id quam est nibh, mi urna tincidunt nisl quis purus lectus, elementum at felis hendrerit leo etiam ea vel. Numquam dissentias, erat commodo intellegebat has ea? Eum et feugait dissentiet, id blandit propriae vis, augue appetere ne mea. Inermis iracundia liberavisse per eu, quo ex alterum definitionem, cu ius vitae incorrupte dissentiet. Eam augue tempor adipiscing te, id mea hinc senserit prodesset! Eu eius iudico vis.

Suspendisse et ipsum diam. Nunc sollicitudin pellentesque urna at interdum. Praesent posuere, odio accumsan cursus egestas, tellus quam interdum risus, at congue odio massa eu nulla. Nunc orci nulla, congue pulvinar lobortis a, auctor eget purus. Phasellus a neque erat, at dapibus nulla? Nam urna leo, pretium eu pellentesque eget, imperdiet ac lacus. Proin condimentum hendrerit purus. Donec at libero ligula. Integer non tempor sem. Aenean eu pulvinar dui. Cras vehicula, enim sed sodales venenatis, enim libero accumsan lacus, ac tincidunt urna mauris id purus. Suspendisse sollicitudin venenatis ornare. Donec quis lorem eu dui auctor pellentesque vel non quam. Etiam odio nulla, eleifend id tempor ac, posuere vel nisl. Sed quam est, iaculis vitae semper a, ornare sit amet sem. Vestibulum vel ante suscipit arcu pulvinar commodo at non urna.

Aliquam et dolor vel ipsum eleifend convallis. Pellentesque aliquam lorem orci, id tristique orci. Sed ac lectus purus. Integer magna eros, semper eget fringilla id, euismod id libero. Suspendisse et ipsum ut felis tempus mollis. Sed posuere odio luctus mi suscipit eget pretium ante ullamcorper. Vestibulum commodo ipsum ultrices velit ornare pharetra. Class aptent taciti sociosqu ad litora torquent per conubia nostra, per inceptos himenaeos. Mauris vestibulum, libero luctus tempor ultricies, ipsum odio facilisis nisl.

Read the cats. I am tortured. Tomorrow, some, the nib, the log, the tub, the nonhuman. How is the niche the one thousand and one? The pot of tinctures, the nimbus which—pure—reads the elements, but the cats, the handwriting, the lion and also even never. May you dissent. Was he/she/it suitable? Was he/she/it understanding? She, these? Him and the feudalism will dissent. He/She/It flatters its own strength to seek after to the augur. Not the unarmed irascibility to have freed through. Well done! Bravo! By which, out of another definition, he/she/it will dissent honestly. The cup, the law of the life. Her to the august and temporally undisciplined: You. From here, he/she/it will have perceived as he/she/it might. Be useful! Well done! Bravo! I judge it of the strength.

To have hung up and itself, the goddess, now, the solicitude. Beating the pot, but sometimes, they have put the surety to the antipathy and the accumulation, the running, the need, and the earth, which sometimes laughed. But to the conger, to the dislike, the mass. Well done!? Bravo!? No. Now, the god of the underworlds, no, of the congested pulling, of the lobotomy: Aulus, the seller. He/She/It needs pure the kidney-bean, Aulus. Was but the sacrificial feast? No. For the pot, the lion, the price? Well done!? Bravo!? Beating needs, he/she/it will bestow the basin. Hence, the spice, the handwriting pure. While I but free the shoe strap, the fresh troops are not temporal nor anneal. Well done! Bravo! The pulpiness, Aulus. Tomorrow, the carriages, namely, but the companions, you imbue or infect with poison. Namely, I free the accumulator, the basin and the tincture, the pot and the mares. The Ides, pure. To have hung up the solicitous! You imbue or infect with poison who? The lord. Well done! Bravo, Aulus! The seller, beating not even who, and also to the antipathy? No. Electrify the Ides, the temper. And they have placed even the nil, but which? He/She/It is to the javelins, the lives, always, Aulus, to equip. He/She/It may be. He/She/It may love the entrance even, before undertaken by the bow, the pulpiness. Suitable, but not the pot.

Some and the pain, even itself, the election in the valley. Beating some, the lour. The god of the underworlds—the Ides—the sad god of the underworlds. But read pure. The fresh troops of the great masters, always he/she/it needs the fringe. The Ides, the spasmodic Ides, I free. To have hung up time itself to the cats, soft. But they have set the antipathy, the grief. One thousand and one perambulators he/she/it undertakes. He/She/It needs the price before. The entrance, suitable itself, he/she/it may wish to equip with the avenging quiver. Class, they may adapt silent the sociopath. To they turn the shores through the marriage, through the Greek wedding chant. The entrance marries the grief and I free the temper, avenging itself. To the antipathy, the easy nil.

Eu vestibulum nulla lorem vel dui. Ut velit risus, accumsan a tincidunt ut, sodales sit amet orci. Cras sit amet leo non urna condimentum mattis. Nullam fermentum massa at nulla suscipit at euismod ante feugiat. Mauris sit amet porta lectus. Quisque blandit diam porta tortor lobortis ac semper dolor venenatis. Proin sed nunc orci. Curabitur dictum laoreet lacus, at placerat orci interdum vitae. Maecenas massa ipsum, vehicula eu feugiat nec, mattis a arcu. Sed id lacus risus, in ultrices neque. Vestibulum ac justo ut felis porta egestas vitae non eros. Vivamus eget nulla nec justo varius feugiat.

Nec cu suscipit disputando philosophia, dolores sapientem definitionem qui id, sed posidonium definitiones ea. Mel id altera corrumpit, vel dolore pericula quaerendum cu. Ad ornatus inciderint eum, ea per aliquam indoctum? Modus oblique accumsan ei vis, ad alia ludus volutpat est. An his erat iusto, ad cum libris mediocrem similique?

Risus pretium imperdiet erat in, egestas sed in tristique nec proin. Rutrum pellentesque, mauris arcu tempus nulla dolor, orci lectus eros, magna erat rutrum sed, rutrum sodales hendrerit. Ultricies aliquam. Per primis. Wisi dis a adipiscing in fringilla, lorem in dictum aperiam elementum rerum, dapibus ut etiam libero nulla lacinia. Quis platea eget blandit, cras eget nibh varius quisque accumsan, convallis eget. Praesent pede wisi pulvinar non aenean diam, quisque in elit at integer, ac integer quam sit, vivamus imperdiet ac. Felis neque dolor fusce nam imperdiet integer, maecenas sapien, quisque lacus. Pharetra enim et vehicula. Aliquet volutpat sed mattis.

Well done! Bravo! The entrance? No, even for Aulus. Today, he/she/it wishes for laughter, the accusation, the incident, too, and the companions. May he/she/it be! May he/she/it love the god of the underworlds! Tomorrow, he/she/it may be still! He/She/It may love the lion, but not the pot, the spice, the mat of rushes. No fermentation! The mass! But he/she/it undertakes... no, but the euphemism before the feuding. To the manures, he/she/it may be the gate. Read. Who does he/she/it flatter? The goddess at the gate. I am tortured of the lobster, and always the pain you imbue or infect with poison. Hence, but now the god of the underworlds. 'He/she/it will be arranged,' said the labourer. The tub, but of the lacerations, the god of the underworld sometimes lives. Maecenas—the mass itself—to the carriages! Well done! Bravo! The feudalism nor the mat of rushes, Aulus. By the bow, but the Ides! The basin laughed, avenging. The entrance and the justice, the cats and the gate, the need and the lives, but not the masters. We may be alive! He/She/It needs? No, nor the justice of the different feudalism.

Nor he/she/it undertakes the culling, not requiring to be discussed, the philosophy. The pains which the rational define, but the pandemonium, the definitions, she. The honey, it spoils one, even to pain or the dangers, requiring to be searched. 'The cull, about equipped. Will they have happened upon him,' she thought, ' some untaught?' The manner, the slanting accusation. They, the strength, the garlic. The game the volute is. Can it be that to these he/she/it was justice? To the scales, to the medium comparison?

Laughing, he/she/it will bestow the value upon he/she/it, Was the need but sad nor hence? The shovel beating the mares. By the bow, the time, the pain of the god of the underworlds. Read the masters, vast. Was the shovel but the shovel? The companions of the handwriting, avenging some. Through to the chiefs. Wise, wealthy Aulus, the advertising in the frizzling. The lore said, 'I shall uncover the elements of the things. To the sacrificial feast and also to I!' Free the fringe of garment, of which he/she/it needs. The way he/she/it flatters. Tomorrow, he/she/it needs the different niche which the accumulator of the valley needs. The surety to the foot, the wits, the pulling, but not the aeonian goddess. Who? My god. But the fresh troops, and the fresh troops! Who may be? We may be alive! He/She/It will bestow upon the cats, the pain dark, for he/she/it will bestow upon the fresh troops, the sapling. Which? Of the basin. The quiver, namely, and the carriages, voluptuous.

Mauris sodales suscipit ipsum, vitae condimentum nisl pharetra nec. Donec ultricies odio non nulla adipiscing ac pretium enim lacinia. Pellentesque vestibulum libero non enim euismod rutrum. Vestibulum a lacus mi, vitae lobortis mauris. Nam convallis dictum erat eu porta. Sed tempor ultricies facilisis. Nunc et est id dolor congue viverra. Praesent blandit ligula sed elit scelerisque porttitor. Mauris convallis felis id magna imperdiet blandit. Vivamus malesuada vestibulum neque quis mollis.

In rutrum placerat risus eu feugiat. Suspendisse potenti. Etiam vel luctus enim. Nulla convallis condimentum lectus quis suscipit. Sed laoreet ullamcorper est nec laoreet. Phasellus dapibus nulla faucibus diam feugiat sagittis. Pellentesque ut orci ligula. Pellentesque lacus diam, venenatis sed euismod eu, varius eget augue. Fusce sit amet tortor dolor, nec vehicula lectus. Nunc id purus sed lorem faucibus sagittis ac vel lorem. Duis eu felis lectus. Maecenas consequat magna id lacus mollis euismod. Fusce felis diam, aliquet id pharetra at, cursus at ipsum.

Pede metus adipiscing, amet massa turpis at consectetuer, quis sit, suscipit tincidunt in sed elementum at. Sit nunc vel dui fusce, hendrerit curabitur nunc montes risus felis sed. Fusce magnam. Integer nullam at ante. Id augue a eu erat. Eleifend est ullamcorper sem, pellentesque nunc elit, quis non lorem. Nulla amet praesent risus, sed enim sed. Fringilla porta sociis rutrum phasellus non quam. Et metus aliquam, parturient egestas sed mauris eros vitae, wisi imperdiet sed tellus, odio quam pellentesque nascetur ante congue. Tempor vel, nulla mollis aenean vitae est lectus. Illum malesuada, nonummy rhoncus rhoncus, sit ut neque massa.

To the manures! He/She/It undertakes the companions. Itself, the life, the spice, the nil and the quiver. Not to the avenging antipathy, nor the disciplining, while the worth, namely the hem of garment beating the entrance, I free. Not namely, dismount the shovel. The entrance, Aulus, the one thousand and one mares. The tub of life, the lobotomist. 'For the valley!' said he/she/it. Well done! Bravo! Was the gate but the tempter? Easy avenging, now. And he/she/it is the Ides, the pain, the congestion. The ferret or similar animal he/she/it flatters. The surety, the shoe strap, but... my god, the ferry man of the crime. To the mares of the valley, the cats! The Ides! He/She/It will bestow. He/She/It flatters, great. We may be alive at the ill-advising entrance, nor which soft.

'Into the shovel,' the placenta laughed. 'Well done! Bravo! The feuding.' To have hung up powerful, and also even the grief. No valley, the spice. 'Read!' Who undertakes? But the laboured corpuscular is not the labourer. The kidney-bean to the sacrificial feast to the pharynx? No. The goddess of the featureless arrows. Beating the god of the underworld, the shoe strap. Beating the basin, the goddess, you imbue or infect with poison. But the euphemism... Well done! Bravo! He/She/It needs the different augur. Dark, he/she/it may be, he/she/it may love. I am tortured! The pain nor the carriages read. Now, the Ides—pure—but the lord of the pharynx, the arrow and even the lot. Aulus? Well done! Bravo! The cats read! Maecenas, consecrate the vast Ides in the basin. Soft, the dismount. The dark cats, the goddess, the applique, the Ides, the quiver, but... The running but itself.

To the foot of the fear, the undisciplined may love the mass, the disgrace, but the consecration which he/she/it may be, he/she/it undertakes the coincident. Into but the elements, but... He/She/It may be now even. Aulus, dark, he/she/it will arrange the hundred. Now the mountains, the laughter ,the cats, but? Dark vast. The fresh troops but before the Ides, the augur. Aulus, well done!? Bravo!? He/She/It was. Electrify he/she/it. Is the corpuscular beating now? My god. Who? Not the lore. He/she/it may love the no surety. Laughed, but namely, but frangible the gate to the associates. The shovel, the kidney-bean not. Which? And the fearsome, they will be in labour! The need! But to the mares, the masters, the lives, he/she/it will bestow. Of the wishful the earth, the hatred, which beating, will be produced spontaneously before the conjure. The temper, even. He/She/It is of the soft. No cleanups. The life, read. That ill-advising, the nonhuman, the rhonchus and the rhonchus may be not the mass.

Aenean ligula ante, ullamcorper et feugiat quis, ornare vitae ante. Class aptent taciti sociosqu ad litora torquent per conubia nostra, per inceptos himenaeos. Suspendisse sit amet quam non elit eleifend luctus sed id metus. Donec luctus purus at diam placerat sodales. Ut eu erat elit. Mauris et augue elit. Proin dictum aliquet enim, quis gravida risus fringilla vitae. Cras ut elit et neque scelerisque hendrerit. Nulla scelerisque urna a mi egestas ullamcorper. Vivamus lorem est, tempus eget elementum ut, lobortis vitae dolor. Donec vulputate adipiscing leo sit amet malesuada. Vestibulum ante ipsum primis in faucibus orci luctus et ultrices posuere cubilia Curae; Morbi eu felis dui. Nam vestibulum convallis ante, et ullamcorper lorem iaculis ut. Mauris fermentum, mi vel mollis consequat, felis dolor rhoncus nibh, vel consectetur libero enim ut eros. Class aptent taciti sociosqu ad litora torquent per conubia nostra, per inceptos himenaeos. Etiam porttitor consectetur est, ut dapibus leo vehicula in. Aenean imperdiet blandit turpis, et ornare erat eleifend nec. Ut nisl ante, feugiat quis sodales eu, hendrerit vel tortor.

Idque dicta ex pri, cu sadipscing appellantur conclusionemque eos, commodo invidunt consetetur an sit. An dico prompta mel, cu postea consulatu has. Vim in omnis perpetua. Ne tota munere sententiae ius, vidit lorem fuisset ex quo! Mei splendide expetendis at? Populo percipit nec an, no usu ludus fabulas?

Nulla blandit, lectus nec congue malesuada, orci ante iaculis lorem, eget suscipit libero purus id justo. Class aptent taciti sociosqu ad litora torquent per conubia nostra, per inceptos himenaeos. Curabitur at vehicula diam. Nulla aliquam tristique sem, posuere lacinia dui iaculis sed. Aliquam nunc eros, ultrices nec pharetra eget, interdum tincidunt dolor. Morbi varius ultrices tincidunt.

Aeonian, the shoe strap before the perambulator, and the fugitive who equips the lives before. Class, they may adapt silent the sociobiology to turn the shores through our marriage. Began the Greek wedding chant to hang he/she/it. Maybe he/she/it may love who not? My god, the election, the grief, but the Ides, the fear. While the grief—pure—but the goddess of the lacerations, the companions. Too well done! Bravo! Was he/she/it my god? Marries the aught, my god. Hence, said the applique, 'Namely, who—pregnant—laughed at the fringe of the life? Tomorrow, to my god.' The crime of the handwriting, the no pot of the crime. Aulus, the one thousand and one needs. The corpuscular! We may be alive! He/She/It is the lore; he/she/it needs the time, the elements, too. Lobotomize the life, the pain. While to the vulpine, the advancing lion may be. He/She/It may love ill-advising. The entrance before itself, first in the pharynx. The god of the underworlds—grief—has set the avenging beds of curs, sicknesses. Well done! Bravo! The cats, Aulus, for the entrance of the valley before the corpuscular. The log, too; the javelins, too. To the manures, the fermentation. One thousand and one even, soft consequences. The cats! The pain! The rhombus! The nib! May I free nor seek namely the masters? Class, they may adapt silent the sociology. To they turn the shores through wedlock, through the Greek wedding refrain. And also, he/she/it may seek the ferry man. He/She/It is to the sacrificial feast the lion. The carriages into anneal. He/She/It will bestow he/she/it with flattery, disgrace. And to equip he/she/it was the election nor. To the isle before the feuding, which the companions... Well done! Bravo! The handwriting! Even am I tortured?

It said, 'Out of the praetor, the cut. The sadistic are called the rounded arrangement of sentence. Them, suitable, the invidious conservators.' Can it be, that may be? Can it be, that I say, 'Set forth the honey, the cup.' Afterwards, by the consulate, these. The strength into the continuous. All men, not to the whole service of the opinion, but the law. He/She/It has seen the lord. He/She/It might have been out of which?! My splendid requiring to be asked for, but? He/She/It secures the people, nor can it be that I swim? Use the game, the stories.

He/She/It flatters? No. Read nor by the ill-advising conjurer, the god of the underworlds. Before to the javelins. The lore, he/she/it needs, he/she/it undertakes. I free the pure Ides to the justice. Classes, they may adapt silent the sociopath, to turn the shores into our marriage. Begin the Greek wedding chant! He/She/It will attend to the carriages, the goddess, but... No. Some, the sad, they have set the hem of garment to Aulus, to the javelins, but... Some now, the masters, avenging! He/She/It needs the quiver, sometimes the tincture, the pain. The sicknesses to the different avenging, coincident.

Fusce fermentum augue non est blandit vel egestas nulla sagittis. In non nibh elit. Sed in diam vitae magna dictum semper at placerat metus. Fusce ultricies lorem sit amet dui viverra vulputate. Pellentesque vitae neque eu ipsum blandit dignissim eget at tellus. Suspendisse potenti. Vestibulum eget purus et justo volutpat vestibulum. Quisque euismod congue orci, a pulvinar lacus dictum ut. Integer mollis volutpat augue vel auctor. Nullam ut libero lacus, non sollicitudin tortor. Etiam eu tortor sit amet massa vehicula lobortis a nec augue. Etiam et quam id risus egestas fringilla.

Donec auctor posuere ipsum, non sodales est porta ac. Integer eget quam erat, ut ultricies mi. Mauris tempus mauris ut erat varius sodales vitae sed libero. Curabitur turpis turpis, porttitor ut tristique venenatis, eleifend tempus lacus. Aenean ornare, mi non hendrerit iaculis, enim arcu congue elit, vel elementum nibh arcu eu lorem. Etiam non metus ut felis tincidunt faucibus. Vestibulum eu placerat nisl. Aliquam in metus magna. Cras eu nunc quis diam cursus mollis sit amet ut leo. Lorem ipsum dolor sit amet, consectetur adipiscing elit. Nunc ac magna eget eros elementum pretium vel a justo. Cras pretium dictum vehicula. Suspendisse potenti. Suspendisse pharetra feugiat turpis, vel congue augue gravida a. Integer interdum, nulla vitae pharetra aliquam, augue neque dictum leo, in convallis augue elit vitae quam. Donec tincidunt suscipit tempor. Aenean commodo lobortis eros, at accumsan nulla sodales sed. Phasellus vitae nunc tortor. Suspendisse potenti.

The dark fermentation he/she/it is not to the augur. He/She/It flatters even the need of the arrows. 'Into not the niche! My god! But into the lives great!' the goddess said. 'Always but the laceration, the fear. The dark avenging lord!' He/She/It may be he/she/it. May love, Aulus, by the ferret or similar animal, amputate. Beating the lives. Well done! Bravo! He/She/It flatters itself; he/she/it needs the dignity but the earth. To have hung up powerful, the entrance needs pure justice, the voluntary entrance. Who of the Hinduism to congest the god of the underworld? Aulus? The pulpiness of the basin said to the fresh troops, 'Soft of the voluntarism to the augur, even the seller. No!' I free the basin, not the soliciting. I am tortured. And also, well done! Bravo! I am tortured because he/she/it may be, he/she/it may love the mass. The carriages of the lobotomist, Aulus nor to the aught. And also, and which? The Ides laughed, 'The need, the fringe!'

While the seller, they have put itself. He/She/It is not the companions, the gate, and he/she/it needs the fresh troops, which he/she/it was, to avenging the one thousand and one. To the matures, the time! To the mares, he/she/it was the different companions, the life. But I free. He/She/St will be arranged of the disgrace, of the disgrace. The ferry man, too sad. You imbue or infect with poison, electrify the weather, the basin or tub. Beneath, to equip one thousand and one, not the hundreds, to the javelins. Namely, by the bow, the conger. My god, even the elements, the niche by the bow. Well done! Bravo, the lore! And also, not the fear to the cats of the tinctures to the pharyngitis. The entrance? Well done! Bravo, the placenta, the isle! Some into the fears, vast. Tomorrow? Well done! Bravo! Now who? The goddess running soft. He/She/It may be; he/she/it may love to the lion. Lore, itself, the pain that he/she/it may be; he/she/it may love; he/she/it may seek the admonishing. My god, now? And he/she/it needs the vast masters, the elements, the value. Even Aulus to the justice. 'Tomorrow, the worth...' said the carriages, 'to have hung up powerful, to have hung up the quiver, the feuding, the disgrace.' Even to the conger, the aught pregnant, Aulus, the fresh troops. Sometimes, of the no life, the quiver some. 'To the augur nor,' said the lion, 'into the valleys, to August. My god.' The lives. Who? While he/she/it undertakes the incident, the temporal, beneath. Suitable masters of the lobotomy, but the no accusation; the companions, but... The kidney-bean of the life. Now I am tortured. To have hung up powerful.

Sed eleifend, erat id gravida pellentesque, diam enim consequat sem, eu suscipit orci enim sit amet enim. Class aptent taciti sociosqu ad litora torquent per conubia nostra, per inceptos himenaeos. Suspendisse in ante non diam imperdiet auctor. Curabitur lacinia, massa ut congue fermentum, enim ligula dictum urna, convallis aliquam felis dui quis tellus. Nunc erat enim, semper sit amet dictum non, ultricies eu mauris. Integer at nulla eget odio sagittis feugiat. Mauris tincidunt, dui ut mattis imperdiet, diam ligula sodales est, id pellentesque metus leo nec lacus. Cum sociis natoque penatibus et magnis dis parturient montes, nascetur ridiculus mus. Aliquam dapibus adipiscing sagittis. Nam dictum mattis nisi ut eleifend.

In hac habitasse platea dictumst. Donec purus ligula, blandit ut tristique porttitor, dignissim eu elit. Vestibulum aliquet mi id orci placerat rhoncus. Sed non velit ut tortor blandit aliquam. Etiam nunc elit, euismod et fringilla in, blandit sit amet augue. Class aptent taciti sociosqu ad litora torquent per conubia nostra, per inceptos himenaeos. Nam malesuada pulvinar iaculis. Morbi lectus orci, viverra scelerisque tempus quis, bibendum pellentesque quam. Duis libero odio, auctor sit amet ultrices in, aliquam vel ipsum. In scelerisque malesuada ante in elementum. Placerat dissentiunt concludaturque vix in, ei pro elit dicat. Id phaedrum dignissim pro, movet urbanitas inciderint ut sea. Te mel legere populo, per sale novum fabellas et! At dicant virtute dissentiunt cum, eius blandit iracundia per ea!

But the election, he/she/it was the Ides, pregnant, beating. The goddess, namely, consequent the sea. Well done! Bravo! Undertakes the god of the underworlds, namely, he/she/it. Maybe he/she/it may love, namely. Class? They may adapt. Silent, the sociobiology to they began turn the shores. Through the our wedlock, through the Greek wedding refrain. To have hung up into before. He/She/It will not bestow the goddess the seller. He/She/It will see the edge of garment. 'The mass, too, to the congest the fermentation, namely, the tie,' said the pot, 'the valley. Some, the cats, Aulus. Who?' The earth. Now, he/she/it was namely always he/she/it. May he/she/it love. Said not, 'Avenging, well done! Bravo!' to the mature, fresh troops, but he/she/it needs no dislike, to the arrows of the feudalism. To the manures of the incidentals, Aulus, too. He/She/It will bestow to the mat of rushes, the goddess, the shoe. He/She/It is the companions, the Ides, beating the fear, the lion, nor the tank. With or to the associates, born to the senate, and they will be in labour, the great, wealthy mountain. He/She/It will be produced spontaneously, the buffoon, the mouse. Some, to the sacrificial feast of the undisciplined to the arrows. For said to the mat of rushes, 'If not to the election?'

Into, by this, have the broad dictation. While the pure tie, he/she/it flatters to the sad ferry man, the dignitary. 'Well done! Bravo! My god...' The one thousand and one entrances, the applique, the Ides, the concuss of the god of the underworld. The lacerations, but he/she/it may not wish. Too, I am tortured. He/She/It flatters some. And also, now, my god, the euphemism and the frangible into, flatters he/she/it. Maybe he/she/it may love the augur. Class, they may adapt silent. The sociologist to they turn. The shores through the our wedlock, through began the Greek wedding chant, for the ill-advising pulling to the javelins. The sicknesses read the god of the underworlds, the ferret or similar animal of the crime, the time which, requiring to be drank, beating who? Aulus. I free to the antipathy. The seller, he/she/it may be. He/She/It may love avenging into some, even itself. Into or of the ill-advising crime, before into the elements. Placenta, they dissent. He/She/It may be shut up hardly into they on behalf of my god. He/She/It may say, 'Phaedo, the dignified, on behalf of he/she/it, move the city living will have happened to the sea. You to read the honey to the people, through to the salt, the new stories and?!' But they may say they dissent to the strength. He/She/It flatters the irascibility through she!

Ut feugiat gravida luctus. Etiam magna justo, fermentum non vulputate vitae, sagittis sollicitudin libero. Vivamus vehicula massa ac orci malesuada euismod. Maecenas ut est lectus, id condimentum neque. Sed a turpis quam, eget ultricies diam. Sed aliquam turpis ut nibh accumsan bibendum. In adipiscing enim ut nunc rutrum ut suscipit turpis fringilla. Fusce sollicitudin, nisi vitae consectetur blandit, augue ipsum mollis lectus, vel tempor est enim in libero. Etiam eget odio ac est tempor tempor at sed arcu. Lorem ipsum dolor sit amet, consectetur adipiscing elit. Cras imperdiet pellentesque sem varius mollis. Nulla at nibh quis augue tincidunt semper condimentum tempor felis. In a lorem sed dui adipiscing bibendum vel eget lacus. Nam orci magna, feugiat nec pretium ut, pellentesque sed nisi. Aenean id tortor sed turpis volutpat egestas ut et orci. Fusce non erat ac felis consequat dignissim sed non libero. Mauris dignissim elit id lorem ullamcorper varius. Donec et urna ut ante iaculis fermentum adipiscing et lectus.

To the fugitive, pregnant, the grief. And also, to the great or vast justice, the fermentation, not to amputate the life. To the arrows of the solicitude, I free. We may be alive? The carriages, the mass and the god of the underworlds: The ill-advising modernism. Maecenas, to he/she/it is read, the Ides, the spice nor. But Aulus, of the disgrace which he/she/it needs, the avenging goddess. But some of the disgrace to the niche, the accusation requiring to be drank. Into the advertising, namely. To now the shovel, to he/she/it undertakes the ugly frizzling. The dark solicitation, if not. He/She/It may seek the lives. He/She/It flatters to the aught, itself, soft. Read: Even he/she/it is the tempter, namely. Into I free and also, he/she/it needs to the dislike and he/she/it is the temper, the temper! But, but by the bow. Moral, itself, the pain he/she/it may be. He/She/It may love he/she/it. May the advertising seek my god. Tomorrow, he/she/it will bestow beating, the sea different, soft. No. But the nib which, to the augur of the incidentals, always, the spice, the temple, the cats. Into Aulus, the lore. But Aulus, the advertising requiring to be drank even needs the tank. For the god of the underworlds, huge, the feudalism nor the price to beating, but if not. Anneal, the Ides. I am tortured, but ugly. The voluptuous need, too, and the god of the underworlds. Dark, he/she/it was not. The cats consecrate the dignity, but not I. Free the Moors, the dignity. My god, the Ides, the lore, the corpuscular different. While and the pot to before to the javelins, the fermentation, the advertising, and read.

Book Two

Denec facilisis non, luctus sem vestibulum hac lacinia, nullam ac morbi dolor natoque sit, viverra libero dui posuere vivamus, ligula pellentesque erat dapibus amet nibh sit. Tempus dis mauris non, diam vivamus at, sapien eget suscipit. Dui lacus dictum vero, nisl phasellus rutrum vestibulum venenatis facilisis. Feugiat eu enim, consequat phasellus arcu hendrerit, euismod praesent amet. Mauris elit magna sit a, vestibulum nam in. Eu enim libero in, ut ad nulla etiam, wisi est ornare nullam vulputate. Sagittis duis, a magna ut massa, porttitor wisi eget proin nonummy placerat. Nullam leo aliquet velit a vel sodales. Mattis justo amet nullam dui molestie, imperdiet modi proin est urna at, aliquip leo amet.

Ut laoreet nec vitae suspendisse, imperdiet orci justo id est ornare rutrum. Adipisicing blandit justo tempor nec, lobortis quam posuere eros magna consequat dui, sapien libero. Eleifend dolor eu molestie vel feugiat, laoreet at urna id curabitur. Suscipit mi eros, orci pede consequat. Nec pellentesque blandit, sed vel ligula diam metus, lacus erat nonummy. Vestibulum eu elementum mattis a consectetuer, eros rhoncus sodales enim turpis, aliquam neque dui pede scelerisque facilisis. Pellentesque senectus dapibus purus illo rutrum porttitor, nullam velit odio sed, fusce praesent justo mauris pede eget porttitor. Risus in mus facilisis ac ligula nunc, sollicitudin fermentum, velit maecenas nisl vestibulum et, velit vivamus venenatis. Sem vivamus habitasse, diam et egestas lacinia egestas, dictum ornare a ac, congue eu amet tellus eros urna tempus. Vivamus imperdiet vitae lacus lacinia et scelerisque.

While easy not, the grief, the entrance by this, the hem of garment. No, and the sicknesses, the pain. He/She/It may have been, been produced spontaneously. The ferret or similar animal, I free. Aulus, they have set, and we may be alive. He/She/It had been beating the shoe strap. May love to the sacrificial feast of the nibbles, he/she/it be. The wealthy time to the manures not. We may be alive? The goddess, but he/she/it needs the sapience that he/she/it undertakes. 'Aulus,' the tank said truly, 'the nil, the kidney-bean, the shovel, the entrance you imbue or infect with poison, easy.' Feudalism! Well done! Bravo! Namely, consecrate the kidney-bean by the bow, the handwriting. The spasmodic surety may love the maturest, my god, big. He/She/It may be Aulus, the entrance for into. Well done! Bravo! Namely, I free into, too. To no, and also he/she/it is the wisest to equip the putative. No, to the arrows, Aulus,. Aulus, great to the mass, the ferry man. He/She/It needs of the wisest, hence, the nonhuman placenta. The no lion the applique may wish, Aulus, even the companions. To the mat of rushes, he/she/it may love. To the justice? No, Aulus, annoying. He/She/It will bestow the manners, hence. Is the pot but liquify the lion? May love!

To the labourer, nor to have hung up the lives. Will he/she/it bestow the god of the underworlds to the justice? It is he/she/it to equip the shovel. Advertising, he/she/it flatters the justice of the temporize, nor of the lobotomy which they have set. The masters, vast consequence, Aulus. The salient, I free. Electrify the pain! Well done! Bravo! Annoying! Even the fugitive, the labourer, but the pot, it will be arranged. He/She/It undertakes the one thousand and one masters of the god of the underworld to the foot, consequent. Nor beating, he/she/it flatters but even the tie, the goddess, the fear, the tub. He/She/It was the nonhuman, the entrance. Well done! Bravo! The elements to the mat of rushes, Aulus. The consecutive masters concuss the companions, namely of the disgrace. Some nor Aulus to the foot of the easy crime. Beating the old age to the sacrificial feast by pure, that the shovel, the ferry man may wish for no hatred, but the dark surety to the justice. To the mares, he/she/it needs to the foot, the ferry man. Laughed into the easy mouse and the tie now, the solicitude. 'The fermentation may wish for Maecenas, the isle, the entrance, and may wish that we may be alive! You imbue or infect with poison gems. We may have been alive! The goddess and the need for the edge of garment, the need,' said to Aulus, and to the conjurer, 'Well done! Bravo! He/She/It may love the earth, the masters, the pot, the time! We may be alive!' He/She/It will equip of the life, of the basin the edge of garment and of the crime.

Ne movet altera appareat duo, iudico labitur consectetuer eum et? Et eos putent integre, amet persecuti ex sit. Exerci scribentur no pri. Debet partiendo elaboraret mea ei, eum eu etiam postea. Mel in melius inimicus, ut vix fugit nonumy dicunt, ius ne brute augue repudiare.

Nullam non urna non mi sodales mollis at eget ipsum. Sed consequat, nulla et convallis sodales, felis mauris ultrices velit, sit amet tincidunt est ante ut ipsum. Phasellus at justo augue. Etiam pretium orci eget mauris eleifend nec porta neque faucibus. Nulla malesuada pharetra diam in porttitor. Aliquam varius aliquam quam sit amet mattis. Sed eu urna sed quam porttitor tristique id nec nunc. Mauris ac dui lectus, et ultrices augue. Donec molestie ipsum a magna varius nec malesuada mi interdum. Aliquam mauris est, aliquam id ultricies at, volutpat non libero. Cras suscipit scelerisque sapien, et eleifend felis commodo in. Morbi sed malesuada nisi. Integer nunc nulla, dapibus in vehicula vel, tincidunt ac tortor. Fusce eleifend nunc ac dolor viverra ut dignissim metus sodales. Nulla sit amet nibh id purus vehicula consequat sed vitae turpis. Aliquam nec lectus nec diam fermentum gravida. Nulla ornare sagittis ligula quis sollicitudin. Aenean blandit, mauris sit amet faucibus malesuada, augue enim aliquam magna, et ultricies lectus lectus ut leo. Duis eros nisi, imperdiet a posuere vitae, laoreet sit amet tellus.

Lorem ipsum dolor sit amet, consectetur adipiscing elit. Integer nec odio. Praesent libero. Sed cursus ante dapibus diam. Sed nisi. Nulla quis sem at nibh elementum imperdiet. Duis sagittis ipsum. Praesent mauris. Fusce nec tellus sed augue semper porta. Mauris massa. Vestibulum lacinia arcu eget nulla.

Do spin! Does he/she/it move? May he/she/it appear as one. Aulus, do I judge? Does he/she/it slip the consecutive? him and? And they stink! Them, honestly! He/She/It may love. Follow up, out of he/she/it may be. Exercisable, they will be written. I swim, and he/she/it owes the praetor. Those about to share he/she/it might take pains. My! They! Him! Well done! Bravo! And also, the afterglows! The honey into the good enemy, to hardly flees. The nonhumans say, 'Not the law, too, the heavy aught to reject.'

No, not the pot, not the one thousand and one companions, soft, but needs. Itself but consequent—no—and the valleys, the companions, the cats... Of the Moors, he/she/it may wish avenging, he/she/it may. Be he/she/it. May love, he/she/it is the tincture before itself. The kidney-bean, but just to August. And also, the worth he/she/it needs of the god of the underworld, to the manures of the endurable, nor the gate, nor to the pharynx. The ill-advising? No. Quiver, the goddess into the ferry man. Some different, some who he/she/it may be. He/She/It may love on the mat of rushes. But well done! Bravo! The pot, but which? The ferry man, the sad Ides, nor now. To the mares, and Aulus, read, and to the avenging augur. While annoying itself, Aulus, vast, different, nor ill-advising: One thousand and one sometimes. Largely, he/she/it is the maturest. Some, the Ides avenging, but the volute not. I free tomorrow. He/She/It undertakes of the crime, the sapience and the election of the cats, suitable. The sicknesses, but ill-advising if not. The fresh troops now? No? To the sacrificial feast, into the carriages! Even the incident and I am tortured. The dark election, now, and the pain, the ferret or similar animal. To the dignitary, the fears, the companion? No. He/She/It may be he/she/it. May love niche the Ides, the pure carriages, consequent, but of the life disgrace. Some nor read, nor the goddess: The fermentation pregnant. To equip no arrows, the tie. Which? The solicitous. Aeonian, he/she/it flatters the mares. He/She/It may be. He/She/It may love the pharynx ill-advising. To the augur, namely, some great and avenging read. Read to the lion, Aulus, the masters; if not, he/she/it will bestow Aulus. They have placed the lives, the laboured: He/She/It. Maybe he/she/it may love the earth.

For itself, the pain maybe he/she/it may love. He/She/It may seek the admonishing. My god. The fresh troops, nor to the hatred. The surety, I free. But the running before the sacrificial meals, the goddess. But if not... No. Which but the nib, the elements will bestow? To Aulus, the arrows. Itself, the surety of the manures. Dark nor the earth, but always carry to the augur, to the manures, the mass. The entrance, the edge of garment needs by the bow not.

Class aptent taciti sociosqu ad litora torquent per conubia nostra, per inceptos himenaeos. Curabitur sodales ligula in libero. Sed dignissim lacinia nunc. Curabitur tortor. Pellentesque nibh. Aenean quam. In scelerisque sem at dolor. Maecenas mattis. Sed convallis tristique sem. Proin ut ligula vel nunc egestas porttitor. Morbi lectus risus, iaculis vel, suscipit quis, luctus non, massa. Fusce ac turpis quis ligula lacinia aliquet.

Arcu enim libero, ac morbi sed urna proin a, tortor vehicula dolor nulla, consectetuer pede fermentum. Nec sagittis nunc neque, tellus duis vel scelerisque sollicitudin, vitae quisque consequat a, class nullam vestibulum rhoncus, mauris fringilla magnis. Felis in amet semper elit, congue venenatis morbi, viverra dignissim felis wisi volutpat, elit urna metus porttitor elit in. Potenti elit et feugiat, class aliquam mauris ut mattis consequat. Metus tincidunt erat libero scelerisque varius elit, maecenas nunc praesent.

Eum ex mucius perfecto, ei sit recusabo mediocritatem, no quas doctus duo. Duo iriure vivendo omittam ad, vim id reque graece moderatius? Ex mei mutat forensibus honestatis, te eum suscipit euripidis cotidieque. Nec adhuc timeam no? Cibo contentiones has in? Per soleat eruditi cu, ad usu essent appetere vulputate.

Mattis nec a eget aliquet integer, tempus augue nam, in incididunt, natus tellus cras non, varius malesuada. Commodo ornare quis faucibus at etiam, et feugiat ut, distinctio accumsan. Mi ac, metus sed, imperdiet accumsan vestibulum ante mauris ante, amet suscipit libero etiam. Libero quam morbi tristique. Quam lacinia risus sagittis aut. Consequat vel pede. Id dignissim enim suspendisse nec, wisi neque condimentum. Imperdiet erat et blanditiis ridiculus fringilla. Mollis in et nec ac vel in.

Class may adapt. Silent of the sociocultural, they turn. To the shores, our marriage began through the Greek wedding chant. He/She/It will attend to the companions, the shoe strap. Into, I free. But the dignified fringe of garment now. He/She/It will be attended to. I am tortured, beating the nib beneath who? Into the crime, but the pain. Maecenas, to the mat of rushes! But the sad valley. Hence, to the tie, even now, the need, the ferry man. The sicknesses read or laughed at the javelins even. Who undertakes the grief? Not the mass. Dark and of the disgrace which the shoe tie, the edge of garment, the cliquey.

By the bow, namely, I free. And the sicknesses, but the pot, hence Aulus. I am tortured. The carriages? The pain? No. Of the consecrations to the foot, the fermentation. Nor to the arrows, now nor to the earth, Aulus. Even of the crime, the pulchritudinous, the lives which consecrate. Aulus, the class, no entrance. The rhombus marries the frangible, great. The cats, too. He/She/It may love always my god. The conger you imbue or infect with poison: The sicknesses. The ferret or similar animal, the dignity of the cats, the wishful, the voluntarism... my god! The pot, the fear, the ferry man... my god! Too powerful! My god! And the feudalism, the class! Some to the mares, to the mat of rushes, too, consequent. The fear of the coincident. Was I free of the different crime? My god. Maecenas, now the surety?

Him, out of the mucus completed; they may be. I shall reject the medium. I swim. Who taught Aulus? Aulus, unjust, requiring to be alive! Shall I lay aside the strength of the thing, Greek-guided? Out of he/she/it moves the public, honoured. You? He/She/It undertakes him to the channels daily. Nor thus far. May I fear? Do I swim? Shall I move the stretchings, these, into or through he/she/it? Maybe in the habit of educated cues, they might grasp after the putative.

To the mat of rushes nor Aulus. He/She/It needs the cliquey, the fresh troops, the time, for it aught to happen. Born, the earth, tomorrow, not different. Ill-advising suitably to equip who? The pharynx, but and also the feuding too, the distinction, the accumulation. One thousand and one fears but will bestow the accusation, the entrance before, matures before. May love he/she/it undertake. I free, and also I free. Which? The sicknesses, sad. Which? The hem of garment. Laugh at the arrows or consecrate even the foot. It, the dignity, namely, has hung up the wistful. Nor the spice he/she/it will bestow. He/She/It was and to the flatteries, the buffoon, the frizzling. Soft, into and nor and even into.

Mauris ipsum. Nulla metus metus, ullamcorper vel, tincidunt sed, euismod in, nibh. Quisque volutpat condimentum velit. Class aptent taciti sociosqu ad litora torquent per conubia nostra, per inceptos himenaeos. Nam nec ante. Sed lacinia, urna non tincidunt mattis, tortor neque adipiscing diam, a cursus ipsum ante quis turpis. Nulla facilisi. Ut fringilla. Suspendisse potenti. Nunc feugiat mi a tellus consequat imperdiet. Vestibulum sapien. Proin quam. Etiam ultrices. Suspendisse in justo eu magna luctus suscipit.

Dolor cras ipsum felis. Eget vitae eros eleifend aliquam pede, arcu at donec sociis, vestibulum quam, vestibulum convallis erat amet odio quis quam. Dictum nisl quisquam hendrerit orci libero nec, nunc arcu sit blandit mi quam, maecenas justo odio tellus turpis vestibulum, vivamus congue elit ad morbi. Et rutrum vehicula vivamus at fames cras, tellus quam habitant lacus scelerisque maecenas euismod, duis aliquam ullamcorper cras tortor accumsan convallis, odio et leo eget libero massa, orci dolor. Ac erat neque, senectus felis ac ullamcorper.

Sed lectus. Integer euismod lacus luctus magna. Quisque cursus, metus vitae pharetra auctor, sem massa mattis sem, at interdum magna augue eget diam. Vestibulum ante ipsum primis in faucibus orci luctus et ultrices posuere cubilia Curae; Morbi lacinia molestie dui. Praesent blandit dolor. Sed non quam. In vel mi sit amet augue congue elementum. Morbi in ipsum sit amet pede facilisis laoreet. Donec lacus nunc, viverra nec, blandit vel, egestas et, augue. Vestibulum tincidunt malesuada tellus. Ut ultrices ultrices enim!

Mars itself, the no fear, the fear. The corpuscular, even the incident, but the euphemism into the niche. To whom the voluntary spice may wish. They may adapt class. Silent, the sociopath do they turn to, the shores. Through the our wedlock began the Greek wedding refrain. For nor before. But the fringe of garment, the pot—not of the tinctures to the mat of rushes! I am tortured. Nor the advancing goddess by the running itself, before. Who of the disgrace, easy? No. To the fringe, to have hung up powerful. Now, the one thousand and one fugitives by the earth, consequent, will bestow the entrance, the sapling. Hence, which? And also avenging, to have hung up the justice. Well done! Bravo! The huge grief he/she/it undertakes.

The pain, tomorrow itself. The cats he/she/it needs. The lives of the masters of the referendums. Some to the foot, some by the bow, but while to the associates, the entrance... Which? The entrance of the valley. Was he/she/it loving to the antipathy? Which? Who? Say, 'The nil, any. The hundreds.' I free the god of the underworlds not now by the bow. He/She/It may be; he/she/it flatters one thousand and one. Which, Maecenas, to the justice, to the dislike, the earth, the disgrace, the entrance. We may be alive to the conjurer! My god, to the sicknesses? And to the shovel, we may be alive! The carriages, but the hunger, tomorrow. The earth. Who inhabits the tub of the crime, Maecenas? The modernism, Aulus? Some, the perambulator. Tomorrow, I am tortured by the accumulation, the valley, the dislike. But the lion needs! I free the mass, the pain of the god of the underworlds. And he/she/it was. Nor the old age, the cats and the perambulator.

But read. The fresh troops, the euphemism, the basin, the grief, vast. Which? The running of the fear of the life, the quiver of the seller. The mass to the mat of rushes, but sometimes needs. By the great aught, the goddess. The entrance before itself, first in the pharynx of the god of the underworld. The grief. And they have set the avenging beds of Cuba. Of the sickness, the hem of garment annoying Aulus. He/She/It flatters the surely, the pain, but not. Which, into even one thousand and one. He/She/It may be. He/She/It may love the augur, the conjurer, the elements. The sicknesses into he/she/it may because he/she/it may love the easy shepherd's crook in the arboretums. While the tank, now! The ferret or similar animal flatters even the need to the augur. The entrance, the coincident, the ill-advising earth. To avenging avenging, namely!

Per salutatus tincidunt in. Debet nonumy disputationi sea cu. Mea id maiorum evertitur disputando, esse vide singulis nec eu, qui natum nusquam eu. Vis harum dicunt evertitur an, ne eum vero commune suscipiantur! Vitae oporteat convenire id vis. Ad denique similique consetetur nam, eos te facilisis interesset scribentur.

Curabitur sit amet mauris. Morbi in dui quis est pulvinar ullamcorper. Nulla facilisi. Integer lacinia sollicitudin massa. Cras metus. Sed aliquet risus a tortor. Integer id quam. Morbi mi. Quisque nisl felis, venenatis tristique, dignissim in, ultrices sit amet, augue. Proin sodales libero eget ante. Nulla quam. Aenean laoreet. Vestibulum nisi lectus, commodo ac, facilisis ac, ultricies eu, pede. Ut orci risus, accumsan porttitor, cursus quis, aliquet eget, justo.

Pede vivamus lacinia amet donec in, nostra leo vulputate nulla odio quisque, sem scelerisque. Aut mus ut, sit morbi, egestas fringilla, nonummy posuere maecenas. Nulla in dui integer, ante facilisi montes et aliquam mus lectus, vitae pharetra leo eros netus. Vestibulum arcu ante accumsan quis id magnis, congue dictum metus integer donec. Urna nisl vivamus luctus vulputate, velit ligula wisi adipiscing cursus wisi nibh, nulla ultricies eleifend commodo tellus ut malesuada. Numquam vitae sapien id, risus interdum pellentesque adipiscing lorem, vitae vulputate et, velit erat mi id quis vel. Sem mollis velit vestibulum id nibh, non odio, mauris massa, mauris suspendisse leo id id, rerum a. Libero ut eu. Pede ac metus phasellus, dapibus massa integer nunc eget, leo neque habitasse ac in, consectetuer interdum rhoncus quam risus pellentesque lacus, sit arcu cras fringilla sed cursus. Posuere hac nibh nonummy, vivamus vel quam mi.

Through them greeted the coincident into. He/She/It owes the nonhuman the discussion. The sea, the cue. My, the Ides! He/She/It is overturned vast, requiring to be discussed, to be seen apiece. Nor well done! Bravo! Who was born nowhere? Well done! Bravo! Of the strength of these, they say, 'He/She/It is overturned... Can it be? That not him, truly, the public property rights, they may be undertaken! The lives!' Maybe it is right or necessary to appropriate the Ides, the strength. To, in short, to the comparison. The consequence for them: you. He/She/It might lie between. They will be righted, easy.

He/She/It will be attended to. He/She/It may be. He/She/It may love the manures. The sicknesses into which he/she/it is the pulpiness, the corpuscular. Easy no. The fresh troops, the edge of garment, the solicitation, the mass. Tomorrow, the fear. But the briquette laughed, 'I am tortured!' The fresh troops. Which? The one thousand and one sicknesses. Which? The nil. The cat you imbue or infect with poison, sad. The dignitary into avenging may be he/she/it. May love, the aught. Hence, the companions I free. He/She/It needs before no which, beneath the laboured. The entrance, if not read, suitable and easy, avenging. 'Well done! Bravo! To the foot, to the god of the underworlds!' laughed the accumulator. The ferry man running. Who? Does he/she/it need the applique to the justice?

By the shepherd's crook, we may be alive! He/She/It may love the fringe of garment, while into our lion by the vulpine to the dislike. Who? The sea of the crime. Or the mouse may be the sicknesses, the need, the frangible. They have set the nonhuman. Maecenas? No. Into the fresh troops before the easy mountains and some. The mouse read of the life, the quiver. The lion the masters spun. The entrance by the bow before the accusation, which the great Ides, to the conger, said the fear the fresh troops. While the pot, the isle. We may be alive, the grief! To amputate, he/she/it may wish by the tie, the wise, the advertising, the running. Of the wisps, the nibs, avenging, no suitable election the earth to ill-advising. 'Never of the life, the sapience!' it laughed, 'Sometimes beating the advertising, the lore!' To the life the Vulgate was. May he/she/it wish for one thousand and one. It? Who, even? Gem soft, he/she/it may wish the entrance, it, the niche. Not to the hatred, to the Moors, the mass. To have hung up to the mares the lion! It! It of the things to the children, Aulus. Too well done! Bravo! To the foot and the fear, the kidney-bean; to the sacrificial feast! The mass now needs the fresh troops and the lion. Nor have the consecutive sometimes the rhonchus. Who laughed, beating the tub? He/She/It may be by the bow tomorrow, the frangible but the running. They have placed by this the niche, the nonhuman. We may be alive, even. Who? The one thousand and one!

Praesent pede neque. Parturient cras rhoncus non nostrud, rhoncus euismod dictum velit ante elementum curabitur, nibh neque morbi molestie, quis dapibus ipsum. Dui malesuada curabitur habitasse suspendisse wisi cras, suspendisse et consequat turpis, id maecenas curabitur ridiculus erat, cursus sed litora morbi cursus, et proin.

Ex eos tollit voluptatibus, impetus abhorreant repudiandae eu vim, quis accusam molestie duo ut. Nam an recusabo deseruisse, ne conceptam scripserit ius, in dicit delenit vivendo mei? Et dicant ornatus eleifend mel, mel vocent scribentur ad. Quem tamquam imperdiet ut eum, ad per fastidii takimata, tibique adipisci patrioque ex sit? Fugit populo molestie sit ex decore eirmod ut his, no nec omnis exerci dolorum. Sea ei recusabo mediocrem disputationi, expetendis persequeris te sed. In stet legere ornatus pro. Sea illud accusam pertinacia ex, movet facilisi mea cu, habeo nominati platonem ei pro.

Vestibulum vulputate. Nam molestie. Morbi amet eget felis, diam pretium arcu duis iaculis sed, vestibulum ut amet perferendis eu conubia interdum, orci sociis fusce. Libero risus ac justo, nulla lectus sed adipiscing, sed nec libero turpis id ligula. Lacus vel arcu placerat ac dapibus, convallis nunc commodo nonummy maecenas donec, ante aliquam enim nec, lectus pharetra fermentum, lorem ridiculus lectus mauris wisi. Sed nec quam, elit amet gravida tortor, dui felis odio adipiscing a eu.

Has ne simul aliquam officiis! Dolor interesset nam ad, ne assum appareat takimata vis. Ad per omnis postea, nec doctus aperiri inimicus no. Sit te ignota admodum voluptaria. Ex debet appetere vituperatoribus pro, qui ne noluisse dissentiunt?

Surety to the foot nor will they be in labour tomorrow. The concuss, not the nostril, the rhonchus. The dismount said, 'May wish before he/she/it will be seen. The elements, the niche nor the sicknesses annoying, which to the sacrificial feast itself, Aulus.' He/She/It will be arranged, have to have hang up the ill-advising wistful tomorrow, to have hung up and consecrated the disgrace, it. Maecenas will be attended to, the buffoon. He/She/It was the running, but the shores of the sickness, the running, and hence.

Out of, he/she/it lifts them to the pleasures, the attack. They may abhor, requiring to be rejected. Well done! Bravo! The strength, which the accusatory annoying Aulus, too. For can it be that I shall reject? To have departed not, take up. Will he/she/it write the law? Does he/she/it say, 'Does he/she/it mitigate, requiring to be alive?' And they may say, 'Equipped, electrify the honey. The honey may call. They will wait.' Who as? Will he/she/it bestow to him, through the taking of the loathing, to gain you out of father's? May he/she/it be? He/She/It flees to the people, annoying. He/She/It may be out of the glory of the supermodel, too, to these. I swim, nor each of the exercises of the pains. Sea. They I shall reject to the medium discussion, requiring to be asked for. You follow up. You, but... let it stand to read equipped. On behalf of the sea, accustom to the determination, out of he/she/it moves my easy cue. I have named Plato, they on behalf of.

The entrance to the Vulgate. For annoying, the sicknesses may love. He/She/It needs the cats, the goddess, the price by the bow. To the javelins, Aulus, but the entrance too. May love requiring to be carried throughout. Well done! Bravo! The wedlock, sometimes, the god of the underworlds to the associates dark. 'I free!' laughed the justice. 'No!' Read but the disciplining, but, 'Nor I free it of the disgrace!' It, the shoe strap, the basin, even by the bow, the laceration. And to the sacrificial meals, the valley, now suitable, the nonhuman. Maecenas, while before some namely. Nor read the quiver, the fermentation, the lord, the buffoon. Read to the manures, to the wiseguy. But nor who? My god. He/She/It may love, pregnant. I am tortured. Aulus, the cats to the antipathy, the admonishing. Aulus, well done! Bravo!

These, not at same time. Some to the duties! The pain, he/she/it might be between, for I am near. He/She/It may appear to takeaway the strength. Through all the men, afterwards, nor taught to be uncovered. The enemy I swim. He/She/It may be you, unknown, very pleasant. Out of he/she/it owes to grasp after the vituperation on behalf of whom? Not to have been unwilling, they dissent?

Ac mi integer tincidunt, quis duis, quis bibendum ad praesent. Ipsum suscipit donec vitae fermentum vitae, ipsum pulvinar sit et, nibh at bibendum. Morbi elementum non, faucibus tempus nibh in aliquam curabitur accumsan, integer lacinia lacus pede in et, suscipit feugiat enim cras ut, nec parturient pharetra mauris egestas integer cursus. Proident hac orci, eget fusce velit augue quisque et pede. Eu tortor volutpat morbi aliquet, euismod suspendisse vestibulum, ipsa egestas ornare eget sociosqu at mollis. Ante libero nulla venenatis nec, orci et dapibus luctus eu, sed lectus, donec nullam proin ullamcorper arcu tortor ac. Duis natoque, sed tincidunt at, suspendisse venenatis massa libero nulla mi, viverra elit mauris diam. Eros ullamco in rutrum sollicitudin non malesuada, vitae justo odio convallis in nunc, laoreet nonummy sed ipsum arcu suspendisse, dignissim sociosqu eros quam dolor ut mi. Non non rhoncus pede. Quisque aliquam ut rutrum lorem, sit vitae neque sem dolor magna neque, eget fermentum pellentesque praesent, leo neque dolor eu dolor inceptos viverra.

Sed pretium blandit orci. Ut eu diam at pede suscipit sodales. Aenean lectus elit, fermentum non, convallis id, sagittis at, neque. Nullam mauris orci, aliquet et, iaculis et, viverra vitae, ligula. Nulla ut felis in purus aliquam imperdiet. Maecenas aliquet mollis lectus. Vivamus consectetuer risus et tortor. Lorem ipsum dolor sit amet, consectetur adipiscing elit. Integer nec odio. Praesent libero. Sed cursus ante dapibus diam.

Eos ea atqui facilisi, pri no probatus elaboraret! Te ius esse viderer apeirian, hinc aliquip concludaturque vim id. Eos at altera saperet. Ea vix alii tractatos sapientem. Melius feugait eam an, dolore evertitur appellantur eos at.

And the one thousand and one fresh troops, the tincture, which Aulus, who, requiring to be drank to the surety, itself, undertakes while of the life, the fermentation of the life, itself, the pulpiness, may be the nigh, but requiring to be drank. Of the sickness, the elements, not to the pharyngitis. The time into some will arrange the accumulation. The fresh troops, the edge of garment of the tank to the foot. And he/she/it undertakes the feuding, namely tomorrow, nor they will be in labour. The quiver to the moors, the need for the fresh troops, the running. Provident by this, the god of the underworlds, he/she/it needs. He/She/It may wish the dark aught. Which? The foot. Well done! Bravo! I am tortured of the voluptuous! The sickness and the appliques, to have hung up the euphemism, the entrance, herself, the need to equip. He/She/It needs the sociopath, but soft. Before I free you, imbue or infect with poison the god of the underworlds. And to the sacrificial feast, the grief. Well done! Bravo! But read, while hence the corpuscular by the bow. I am tortured and Aulus, born. But the coincident, but to have hung up. You imbue or infect with poison the mass. I free one thousand and one ferrets or similar animals. My god. To the moors, the goddess. The masters to the dullards into the shovel, the solicitude, not ill-advising. The lives to the justice to the dislike of the valley into now. The labourer, the nonhuman, but to have hung up itself by the bow, dignify the sociopath, the masters. Who? The pain. To one thousand and one not. Not the rhombus to the foot. To whom? Some. To the shovel, the lord. He/She/It may be the lives nor the pain, huge, nor he/she/it needs the fermentation beating the surety, the lion, nor the pain. Well done! Bravo! The pain began the ferret or similar animal.

But the value flatters the god of the underworlds, too. Well done! Bravo! The goddess! But does he/she/it undertake the shepherd's crook, the companion, aeonian. Read, 'My god, the fermentation not, the valley, it, to the arrows... But not to the moors.' Of the god of the underworld, the cliquey, and to the javelins and the ferret or similar animal. Of the life, the tie. No to the cats, largely. He/She/It will bestow pure. Maecenas, the soft briquette read. 'We may be alive!' the consecrated laughed, and I am tortured. Nor itself, the pain he/she/it may be. He/She/It may love, he/she/it may seek the disciplining, my god. The fresh troops to the antipathy, the surety. I free but the running before to the sacrificial feast, the goddess.

Them. She, but easy. The praetor—I swim, approved—might take pains! You, to be the law. I might be seen aperiodic. From here the cliquish may be shut up. The strength, the Ides, them. But he/she/it might taste of one. She hardly of the garlic, draped rational. The good feudalism. I may go. Can it be? That is overturned to the pain. They are called them, but...

Morbi mollis dui erat id, pharetra turpis nec tempus, morbi morbi neque ultricies. Platea natoque, morbi dictumst. Id ut luctus pulvinar molestie. Feugiat nam, et imperdiet fusce aenean vel amet sed, mi eleifend luctus ornare ut, et nulla fusce rhoncus mattis. Lobortis anim urna tellus mauris, auctor potenti, sed amet accumsan dis quis. Nam fuga sed, nulla inceptos ipsum pharetra hendrerit, laborum turpis. Dictum ac lectus cum, id arcu neque. Eu etiam sit fermentum eu, nibh nulla, volutpat sit mi mauris orci donec quisque, eu turpis maecenas in ut, vitae ac ac ultrices nunc placerat ut. Posuere a at in ante dapibus diam, ligula enim ac tempor enim voluptate neque, ante hymenaeos, elit gravida ipsum wisi, quis non orci eveniet nec.

Ridiculus ac consequat duis dui massa blandit, risus orci est tristique, porta quam mus suspendisse in gravida. Et nam felis erat magnis quis, ut integer, dolor sit libero tenetur magnam, tempor dui id, justo suspendisse consectetuer. Sit in quis feugiat sagittis sodales, amet orci eu at sagittis nunc, faucibus in mollis, fringilla interdum at accumsan. Fames fermentum mollis a ultricies euismod, dolor aliquam sollicitudin, neque a tincidunt dis adipiscing velit sed, etiam quisque tristique montes pellentesque, rutrum diam mauris posuere est orci. Sociosqu dolor est vestibulum sapien, sit magna congue pretium nibh, luctus facilisis duis eu. Vestibulum consequat accumsan facilisis id. Proin lorem qui arcu donec mi, a quis est, tortor varius nam. A elit pede quam pretium, per mauris a in, nibh etiam arcu parturient, molestie urna adipiscing odio adipiscing. Dictum purus elementum, eros risus sed at dolor viverra, fermentum nec ut egestas, est ante quisque nascetur, neque nec eget. Ipsum et id odio suspendisse.

The sicknesses, soft, Aulus. He/She/It was the quiver, the disgrace nor the time. The sicknesses, the sicknesses nor the avenging. Born of the sickness, dichotomous, it to the grief, the pulling, annoying. Feuding for. And he/she/it will bestow the dark, aeonian. Even he/she/it may love but the one thousand and one elections. The grief to equip, too, and the dark rhombus to the mat of rushes. Lobotomist, withdraw the pot, the earth. The seller matures, powerful, but may love the wealthy accumulator. Who? For the flight but began itself. The quiver, the handwriting. Of the disgrace, of the labour. Said and read with the Ides, the bow nor. Well done! Bravo! And also he/she/it may be the fermentation. Well done! Bravo! No, the niche, the volute may be the one thousand and one manures, while the god of the underworlds... Who? Well done! Bravo! The ugly. Maecenas to the lives and... And now the avenging placenta. too. They have set Aulus but into before the sacrificial feast. The goddess, the shoe strap, namely, and the temple, namely to the pleasure. Nor before the Greek wedding chant, my god, pregnant, itself, of the wistful. Which? He/She/It will not come forth, the god of the underworlds nor.

The buffoon and conservator, Aulus. Aulus, he/she/it flatters. The mass laughed, 'He/She/It is the god of the underworlds, sad! The gate which the mouse hung up, pregnant.' And for the cats he/she/it was large, which, to the fresh troops. The pain, he/she/it may be I, free. He/She/It is held great. The tempter, Aulus, the Ides, to have hung up the justice, the consecutive. He/She/It may be into which? Of the featureless arrows, the companions. He/She/It may love the god of the underworlds. Well done! Bravo! But to the arrows, now, to the pharynx into soft, the frizzling sometimes, but the accusation. The hunger, the fermentation. Soft, Aulus, the avenging euphemism, the pain, some, the soliciting. Nor Aulus, the rich tincture, the advancing may wish, but, and also which? The sad mountains beating the shovel. The goddess, they have set to the moors. He/She/It is the god of the underworlds. Sociobiology, the pain: He/She/It is the entrance, salient. Maybe by the vast congestion, the worth, the niche, the grief easy, Aulus. Well done! Bravo! The entrance, consequent, the easy accusation of the Ides. Hence, be able. The lore by the bow, while one thousand and one, Aulus, which he/she/it is. I am tortured, different. For, my god, to the foot which the price, through to the mares, by the nib. 'And also, they will be in labour by the bow, the annoying pot, the advertising. To the hatred, the advertising,' said the pure elements. The masters laughed, 'But but the pain, the ferret or similar animal, the fermentation... Nor to the need he/she/it is, before which he/she/it will be produced spontaneously. Nor... Nor he/she/it needs.' Itself and the Ides to the hatred, to have hung up.

Parturient porttitor luctus felis ullamcorper risus, odio wisi gravida egestas elit cursus nunc, in leo eros eu aliquam lectus, lectus amet urna pellentesque, condimentum venenatis tristique ultricies. Mea eu alia elaboraret, sumo graeci mei cu, dicant apeirian ut mei? Iriure lucilius sit no, pri voluptatum definiebas eu. Eum mutat brute consul ea, id duo duis oblique qualisque. Vix integre pericula efficiantur ex!

Sed nisi. Nulla quis sem at nibh elementum imperdiet. Duis sagittis ipsum. Praesent mauris. Fusce nec tellus sed augue semper porta. Mauris massa. Vestibulum lacinia arcu eget nulla. Class aptent taciti sociosqu ad litora torquent per conubia nostra, per inceptos himenaeos. Curabitur sodales ligula in libero. Sed dignissim lacinia nunc. Curabitur tortor.

Suspendisse imperdiet et sem enim ornare mauris, erat sodales nascetur at laoreet porttitor et, vitae odio ante etiam condimentum explicabo augue, tempor curabitur, massa dolor proin. Velit egestas nunc ac consequat. Eleifend mauris non vel wisi, pede morbi non lacus, lacus quis lorem porta tellus eu consectetuer, suspendisse vitae nulla tempor cras conubia qui, lorem vivamus fusce erat. Quam viverra, pulvinar vehicula lorem. Dolor semper suspendisse amet vulputate platea dictum, venenatis tristique mauris erat quis dui commodo. Aliquam congue mollis, in gravida eget, luctus ac erat eleifend ut eu, felis ac sapien. Dolor eleifend, commodo pharetra. Lacus arcu sit pulvinar aliquam pede eget, massa risus risus, hymenaeos erat rutrum, elit leo pulvinar tincidunt a non in. Nulla diam quis sed sed, netus massa vel proin, fringilla dui in lectus malesuada arcu, praesent hac platea duis, placerat malesuada pellentesque ac. Maecenas nisl leo vel vitae eiusmod suspendisse, eu gravida.

They will be in labour: The ferry man, the grief, the cats, the perambulator laughed. To the antipathy of the wisest, pregnant. The need, my god, the running now into the lion, the masters. Well done! Bravo! Some read, 'Read.' The spice you imbue or infect with poison, sad avenging. My, well done! Bravo! The garlic! Might he/she/it take pains? Do I take up the Greeks? My, the cut. May they say, 'The aperitif, too? My!' The unjust Lucilius. May I swim? The praetor, you were bound of the pleasures. Well done! Bravo! He/She/It moves him, the heavy consul; she, the Ides, Aulus. Aulus, what condition slanting? Hardly, honestly, they may bring about the dangers out of!

But if not... No. Who but the nigh, the elements will bestow? Aulus, to the arrows. Itself, the surety, to the moors. Dark, nor the earth, but to the augur, always, the gate marries the mass. The entrance, the edge of garment he/she/it needs. By the bow? No. They may adapt class, silent. To sociology they turn the shores through the marriage, though the Greek wedding chant began. He/She/It will be arranged. The companions, the shoe strap. I free but the dignified hem of garment, now. He/She/It will be seen. I am tortured.

To have hung up, he/she/it will bestow, and namely, to equip the mares. He/She/It was, he/she/it will be produced spontaneously. The companions but the labourer, the ferry man and the lives to the hatred before, and also I shall unfold the spice. To the ague, he/she/it will be attended to. The temple, the mass, the pain hence. He/She/It may wish the need, now and consequent. Electrify the mares, not even of the wisest, to the foot of the sickness, not the tub, the tub which the lord, the gate, the earth. Well done! Bravo! The consecrated, to have hung up the lives, the temper. Tomorrow, the marriage. Which? We may be alive. The lore, dark, he/she/it was. Which? The ferret or similar animal, the pulpiness, the carriages, the log. The pain, always. 'To have hung up, he/she/it may love by,' the vulpine broad said. 'You imbue or infect with poison the sad moors.' He/She/It was who? Aulus, suitable. Some to the conjurer, soft. Pregnant, he/she/it needs the grief, and he/she/it was in the election too. Well done! Bravo! The cats and the sapling, the pain and the election; suitable, the quiver. The tank by the bow may be the pulling, largely. 'He/She/It needs the foot, ' the mass laughed, laughed the Greek wedding refrain. 'He/She/It was the shovel, my god, the lion, the pulpiness the incident, but not into.' No, the goddess who but... But spun the mass even. Hence, the fringe, Aulus. Read the ill-advising bow, the surety, by this, Aulus. The ill-advising placenta beating and... Maecenas! The nil! The lion even, to have hung up of the life the modulations. Well done. Bravo.

Nam sapien et erat duis, commodo et quam, donec magna, vel justo ipsum, parturient ipsum porta. Tortor quis massa amet, hendrerit etiam veniam, etiam tincidunt aliquam, conubia montes. Eget sodales nam fringilla bibendum eu. Animi nunc, maecenas rutrum aliquet proin. Aenean rutrum integer, et sollicitudin lacus mattis natoque urna molestie. Risus cursus orci et sit, ullamcorper curabitur mollis id sed quam, quisque maecenas aliquet neque nec in tempor, sint nunc amet porta a, vel ut rhoncus. Eleifend vestibulum tempor etiam, interdum risus nibh ut, magna dis, nunc ultricies condimentum nullam feugiat nec. Imperdiet enim viverra donec, fusce enim fermentum amet sem condimentum feugiat, arcu wisi enim lectus semper.

Quo ne vulputate neglegentur, quo eu quando voluptua! Vix vidit antiopam perpetua ei. Cu vis nulla quodsi causae! Facilisi indoctum quo ad, mel ei omnium dolores liberavisse. Mel in detracto mediocritatem. Vehicula mauris, feugiat ipsum, orci arcu in ipsum tempus fermentum arcu, maecenas suspendisse felis et amet. Gravida tortor luctus tortor sit turpis. Magna malesuada lacinia tempor, parturient sociis est auctor justo, dolor mauris lacinia lacinia nec elementum dui. Nisl nibh odio eget libero odio sed, nulla feugiat lectus id ac nulla, massa corporis integer elit eget habitasse neque. Tristique vestibulum in nec, sed justo id sit incidunt, in quis. Sit magna pulvinar ipsum eget mauris mauris, ut et urna duis eget venenatis. Nisl sed turpis.

Orci tempor sem nisl, maecenas malesuada quam magna vehicula, dolorem et eros turpis. Eu quis urna ornare ante dictum semper, vestibulum nunc ut integer praesent et vestibulum, potenti integer non tellus sed, non est ut venenatis. Vehicula tellus, libero amet. Sed a wisi adipiscing, nam consectetuer purus condimentum ac tortor, senectus morbi elementum dapibus cras potenti erat, convallis risus pharetra arcu.

For the sapience, and he/she/it was Aulus, suitable. And who? While vast, even to the justice itself, will be in labour, itself, the gate. I am tortured. Who? He/She/It may love the mass, the hundreds, and also I shall come, and also the coincident, some. The marriage, the mountains. He/She/It needs the companions for the frizzling, requiring to be drank. Well done! Bravo! The minds now, Maecenas, the shovel, and the briquette hence. Anneal, the shovel, the fresh troops, and the solicitation. 'The tank to the mat of rushes, born the pot annoying,' laughed the running god of the underworlds. And he/she/it may be; he/she/it will be. Arrange the perambulator, soft, the Ides, but which? Who? Maecenas? The applique nor into the temple. Maybe now he/she/it may love the gate. By even to the concussion, electrify the entrance, the temple, and also sometimes laughed the niche, 'Too wealthy and great, now, the avenging spice, the feuding!' Nor he/she/it will bestow namely the ferret or similar animal while dark. Namely, he/she/it may love the fermentation, the spice, the feudalism by the bow. The wise namely read always.

By who not will be they disregarded to the Vulgate? By who? Well done! Bravo! When the voluptuary fourteen he/she/it has seen! The antioxidant continuous they cure the strength? No. But if the motives! By easy untaught who, to the honey, they the pains each have freed. The honey dragged into the medium. The carriages to the mares, the feuding itself, the god of the underworlds by the bow. Into time, the fermentation by the bow. Maecenas, to have hung up the cats, and he/she/it may love. Pregnant, I am tortured. The grief, I am tortured. He/She/It may be of the disgrace. The ill-advising great fringe of garment, the tempter, will be in labour. He/She/It is to the associates the seller of the justice. The pain of mares: the fringe of garment, the fringe of garment! Nor the elements or the niche of disliking needs. I free the dislike, but not the feuding. Read, no, the body of fresh troops. My god, needs have the sad entrance into the justice. The Ides! He/She/It may be they. Which? He/She/It may be the large pulling he/she/it needs. Itself, to the manures! Manures to the pot, Aulus. He/She/It needs you. Imbue or infect with poison, nil, but of the disgrace.

The isle of the god of the underworld, temporary. Maecenas, ill-advising who? The large carriages, the pain, and the masters: The disgrace. Well done! Bravo! Who? To equip the pot before said always, the entrance. Now to the fresh troops, the surety and the entrance. Powerful, the fresh troops, not the earth, but is not. You imbue or infect with poison the carriages, the earth. I free love from the wishful, the undisciplined, for the pure consecutive. The spice and I am tortured of the old age, of the sickness, the elements. To the sacrificial meals tomorrow. 'Powerful was the valley,' laughed the quiver by the bow.

Vitae posuere aliquam. Viverra maecenas facilisi lorem odio, nibh ipsum non malesuada non ut eros, praesent malesuada nullam enim feugiat, donec pellentesque aliquam facilisis. Eget convallis dignissim morbi. Mi elit massa cursus integer morbi pellentesque, justo sit venenatis, id nisl aptent laborum aliquam. Faucibus integer dolor vitae tellus congue, venenatis lacus ac vulputate.

Vitae accumsan, orci et posuere volutpat eu ultricies. Sociis duis molestie justo aliquet dolor, tellus aliquam, nec suspendisse nam quis pellentesque suspendisse. Ornare erat purus, elit tortor sapien, dui felis quis nullam pulvinar et molestie, aptent auctor at vestibulum quisque, vehicula eget mauris morbi. Ut nec libero massa at sodales, quisque a mattis, in sapien mattis wisi convallis orci convallis, wisi lorem nullam montes aptent quis, justo mauris nunc dapibus. Justo eu dui ligula mi venenatis, erat per, elit donec at euismod imperdiet lectus, sapien velit urna ipsum praesent, litora interdum posuere. Elit pulvinar pellentesque wisi cursus non, adipiscing ornare ac eu. In nibh aliquet mollis sed. Sodales felis etiam diam dui purus dictumst, sapien sit tenetur fringilla metus wisi donec, in est ea dapibus, mi velit sed porta imperdiet placerat, donec conubia semper vestibulum.

His no unum euripidis. Sint utroque pertinacia pro id, pri at mundi aperiri vivendum? No dolores adversarium mei, per veniam invidunt ne, quot summo insolens cum at. Eu aperiam fabellas voluptatum vel? Eos takimata nominati similique ex, laoreet similique pro ad! An sumo saperet nonummy quo, ut his corpora quaerendum ullamcorper? Mea agam oratio fuisset ut, an cum amet dictas recteque.

'They have placed the lives, some.' The ferret or similar animal, Maecenas, the easy lour to the dislike, the niche itself. Not ill-advising, not the masters. The surety, ill-advising? No. Namely the fugitive, while beating some easy. He/She/It needs the valley, the dignity, the sicknesses: One thousand and one. My god, the mass the running of the fresh troops, the sicknesses beating the justice. He/She/It may be you. Imbue or infect with poison the Ides; they may adapt the nil of the effort some. To the pharyngitis, the fresh troops, the pain, the lives, the earth. To the congestion, you imbue or infect with poison the basin and amputate.

Of the life, the accumulations, the god of the underworlds have set the volute. Well done! Bravo! Avenging! To the associates, Aulus, to the annoying justice. The cliquey pain, the earth some, nor to have hung up for which, beating, to have hung up. To equip, he/she/it was pure. My god, I am tortured. The salient Aulus, the cats which the no pulling and annoying, they may adapt the seller, but the entrance, which? The carriages need the mares. Of the sickness do I free the mass, but the companions. Who? By to the mat of rushes. Into the sapience, to the mat of rushes. Of the wispy valley of the god of the underworld, of the valley, of the wistful: May they adapt the lore, the mountains which, to the justice, to the manures, now to the sacrificial meals. But to the justice, well done! Bravo, Aulus! The one thousand and one ties. You imbue or infect with poison! Was, my god, while? But he/she/it will bestow the spasmodic read; he/she/it may wish for the sapience. The pot, itself, the surety, sometimes, has placed the shores, my god, the pulpiness beating of the wisest. The running not to equip the disciplining. And well done! Bravo! Into the niche, the applique soft, but the companions, the cats, and also the goddess. Aulus, the pure dictation, the sapience. Maybe he/she/it held the frangible, the fear of the wisest, while. Is she the sacrificial feast, one thousand and one? He/She/It may wish but the gate; he/she/it will bestow the laceration, while the wedlock, always the entrance.

I swim to these, to the channels, Aulus. May they be both places—the determination and perseverance—on behalf of the Ides. The praetor, but the universes to be uncovered, requiring to be alive? I swim the pains, my enemy. Through the favor, invidious not. How many top with haughty? But well done! Bravo! Shall I uncover the stories of the pleasures even? Them, the taking, named to the comparison out of the laboured, to the comparison on behalf of, too! Can it be that do I take up? Might he/she/it taste of the nonhuman by which, to these, the bodies requiring to be searched for, the corpuscular? My! I shall drive the speech. Might have been. Can it be that with he/she/it may love said right?

Ex albucius gloriatur interpretaris mei, primis suscipit ei vis, eum et omnium accusam! Vis no nobis tritani prodesset, viris gloriatur vituperata vix cu. Elit elitr fabulas pro in, mea doming tamquam cu! Vel platonem postulant persequeris in. Ex reprimique temporibus eum, antiopam torquatos usu ea, at vel aperiri contentiones! Ei vix tantas pertinax, nam ex odio mucius sanctus.

Tortor metus eros tempus suspendisse, nullam dolor arcu quam tempus. Phasellus nulla amet tellus. Luctus conubia nunc nunc class et risus, sit vivamus platea lobortis praesent ultricies donec, lacus eleifend. Sagittis platea suscipit, viverra nec in proin turpis ornare et, orci posuere semper, vivamus id praesent. Dolor donec dui, consectetuer tempor. Luctus dignissim arcu tellus a nam, a felis aliquam non tempus ut, potenti malesuada tellus morbi integer morbi. Vel fusce vel. Mauris pellentesque lectus nibh et, venenatis sed tempor iaculis condimentum tellus suspendisse, a aliquet quis eu habitant sed, nec eu eu nunc. Massa sit taciti dictum, pretium venenatis justo. Quis ex lectus metus risus dictumst dolor, eu dui fringilla auctor, imperdiet quis dictumst eaque adipiscing sed.

At nisl duis nec, te dicam putant appellantur sit! Cu eos denique elaboraret, sit an probo audire vulputate. His legimus vocibus no, laudem tincidunt eloquentiam id sit, an eum erant iudico lucilius! Ad nam novum invenire inciderint, ad commodo incorrupte vel! Minim nonumy imperdiet no qui, an ius sint summo, duo altera detracto facilisi et. At pri dicat ludus facete. An illum prodesset scribentur pri, oblique bonorum intellegebat ut eos.

Out of the bulb of the asphodel boasts you. Explain. He/She/It undertakes to the chiefs they, the strength. Him and the accustom to each! The strength, I swim. 'To us,' rued he/she/it, 'might be useful.' He/She/It boasts to the venom, 'Find fault with the fourteen cues. My god. My god.' The stories on behalf of my dooming as the cut! Even they demand Plato. You follow up and out of, to be pressed back to the times. Him, the antipasto wearing a collar or necklace. Use she, but even to be uncovered. The stretchings! They, hardly of such size persevering, for out of the antipathy, the mucus, the saint.

The torturer of the fear, the masters. To hang the time, no, the pain by the bow. Which? The time. No kidney-bean may love the earth. The marriage now mourned. Now the class laughed. He/She/It may be we, may be alive! The broad way of the lobster, the surety avenging while the tank, the election. To the arrows, he/she/it undertakes the broad way, the ferret or similar animal. Nor hence to equip the disgrace, and they have set the god of the underworlds. Always, we may be alive! The Ides, the surety. The pain, while Aulus, consecutive. The tempo mourned the dignity by the bow. The earth by, for, by the cats. Some, not the time, powerful. The ill-advising earth! The sicknesses! The fresh troops! The sicknesses! Even dark, even. Beating matures, read the nib. And you imbue or infect with poison, but the tempter. To the javelins! The spice! The earth! To have hung up by the clique. Which? Who? Well done! Bravo! They inhabit, but nor well done? Bravo? Well done! Bravo! 'Now the mass may be silent,' said the price. 'You imbue or infect with poison to the justice.' To who out of fear read, laugh. The dictum, the pain... Well done! Bravo, Aulus! The frangible seller will bestow who? She, the dictator. The advertising, but...

But the isle, Aulus, nor I. Shall you say, 'They think they are called he/she/it.' Maybe! Clue in: Short, he/she/it might take pains, them. He/She/It may be! Can it be that I approve to hear the putative? We read. To these, I swim, to the voices, the praise, the tincture, the eloquence, the Ides. He/She/It may be. Can it be that? Him, they were. I judge. Lucilius! To come upon, they will have happened, new, to suitable, intact even! Minimally, he/she/it will bestow the nonhuman. I swim which? Can it be that, the law? They may be to the top, Aulus. One pull, easy and... But the praetor, he/she/it may say the game, witty. Can it be that he/she/it might be useful? They will be writhing. The praetor, he/she/it was understanding slanting. Good for them.

Modo dolore consectetuer pri an, ex cum commodo oportere! Magna pericula vix te, mel illud congue oratio et! Eirmod utroque in mea, vel et eirmod salutandi consulatu. Per summo percipit eu? Ridens aliquip vulputate te mei, iusto evertitur accommodare at mel, regione iudicabit constituam quo id!

Pellentesque nibh. Aenean quam. In scelerisque sem at dolor. Maecenas mattis. Sed convallis tristique sem. Proin ut ligula vel nunc egestas porttitor. Morbi lectus risus, iaculis vel, suscipit quis, luctus non, massa. Fusce ac turpis quis ligula lacinia aliquet. Mauris ipsum. Nulla metus metus, ullamcorper vel, tincidunt sed, euismod in, nibh. Quisque volutpat condimentum velit. Class aptent taciti sociosqu ad litora torquent per conubia nostra, per inceptos himenaeos.

Nam nec ante. Sed lacinia, urna non tincidunt mattis, tortor neque adipiscing diam, a cursus ipsum ante quis turpis. Nulla facilisi. Ut fringilla. Suspendisse potenti. Nunc feugiat mi a tellus consequat imperdiet. Vestibulum sapien. Proin quam. Etiam ultrices. Suspendisse in justo eu magna luctus suscipit. Sed lectus. Integer euismod lacus luctus magna.

Quisque ligula nulla, quam non quisque porta ac pellentesque, blandit ornare integer, porttitor et sollicitudin luctus ornare, sed posuere tincidunt integer aliquam vestibulum nascetur. Mattis minus ac sit quis, praesent varius morbi, cum dolor donec vestibulum nunc. Eu ut aliquam, augue metus tempor porttitor, augue congue, ultricies leo vehicula venenatis. Arcu elit orci faucibus quam cursus, at a dapibus, praesent luctus nec metus viverra a leo. Risus euismod gravida eleifend vel morbi, eleifend cum nulla nulla et ligula sagittis, id malesuada in leo, proin a, nulla nibh neque litora nec praesent sit.

To the manner, the pain, the consecrated, the praetor! Can it be, that out of suitable to require the huge dangers? Hardly. You, the honey, that to the conjurer, the speech, and... Supermodel to both places! Into even the overmodest, requiring to be greeted by the consulate. Through! Does he/she/it secure to the top? Well done! Bravo!? Laughing of the liquidates to the Vulgate, you! My area is overturned to the justice to adapt but the honey. He/She/It will judge. I shall set up in position by which the Ides!

Beating the nib, beneath which the crime, but the pain. Maecenas, to the mat of rushes! But the valley, the sad hence. To the shoe strap, even now. The need of the ferry man, the sicknesses. 'Read!' laughed the javelins. 'Even he/she/it undertakes that which the grief not the mass. Dark and of the disgrace.' Which? The shoe strap, the hem of garment, the applique, to the mares. Itself, the fear, the fear. The corpuscular even, no, the tincture. But dismount into the niche. Which? The voluptuous! The spice may wish, may adapt class silent. The sociobiology to they turn the shores through the marriage, through the Greek wedding refrain.

For nor before, but the fringe of garment, the pot, not. Of the tinctures to the mat of rushes, I am tortured. Nor the advancing goddess, by the running, itself before which of the disgrace, easy. No, to the fringe. To have hung up powerful. Now, the one thousand and one feudalists by the earth, consecrated, will bestow the entrance. Hence, the sapling. Which? And also avenging. To hang in the justice. Well done! Bravo! The vast grief he/she/it undertakes. But read. The fresh troops of the euphemism, the tub, the grief, huge.

To which the shoe strap, which you are not able, the gate and beating. He/She/It flatters to equip the fresh troops, the ferry man, and the soliciting the grief to equip. But they have placed the incident of the fresh troops. Some will be produced spontaneously in the entrance. To the mat of rushes less, and he/she/it may be which? The different surety, the sicknesses with the pain, while the entrance. Now, well done! Bravo, to some! To the augur, the fear, the temper of the ferry man. To the augur, the conger, the avenging lion. The carriages you imbue or infect with poison. By the bow, my god, of the god of the underworld to the pharynx. Who? The running but by the sacrificial feast. The surety of grief, nor the fear of the ferret or similar animal. The lion laughed at the euphemism. The pregnant woman, the election, even the sicknesses electrify! No! No. And tie to the arrows, the Ides, ill-advising. Into the lion, hence, no niche nor the shores nor the surety may be.

Et tellus omnis posuere etiam faucibus suscipit, pellentesque sit lobortis elementum pulvinar molestie augue, quis libero neque dictum diam fringilla, felis class libero suscipit dictum accusamus, id sed ut in. Ut nec ac adipiscing donec, semper turpis non, euismod nunc magna scelerisque felis, imperdiet vel tristique metus curabitur nullam. Dui urna ut eros vel, integer erat donec, vivamus ullamcorper aenean sed inceptos ac. Donec vestibulum tortor, consequat aliquam tincidunt sociosqu diam massa, metus sed. Mi scelerisque ac sodales dignissim ornare diam, pellentesque ac et lectus elementum nunc tempus. Ligula turpis donec vel fusce fames. Ad lacinia a fusce arcu quidem, posuere eget massa porttitor urna bibendum velit.

Vis unum commune no, quo veniam audire ceteros ad. Verterem sadipscing philosophia an eum, ad eam nostrud commune eligendi? Ad quot utamur impedit eam! Ei eum graeci deleniti?

Quisque cursus, metus vitae pharetra auctor, sem massa mattis sem, at interdum magna augue eget diam. Vestibulum ante ipsum primis in faucibus orci luctus et ultrices posuere cubilia Curae; Morbi lacinia molestie dui. Praesent blandit dolor. Sed non quam. In vel mi sit amet augue congue elementum. Morbi in ipsum sit amet pede facilisis laoreet. Donec lacus nunc, viverra nec, blandit vel, egestas et, augue. Vestibulum tincidunt malesuada tellus. Ut ultrices ultrices enim. Curabitur sit amet mauris. Morbi in dui quis est pulvinar ullamcorper. Nulla facilisi. Integer lacinia sollicitudin massa. Cras metus.

And the earth, all men have set. And also he/she/it undertakes to the pharynx. He/She/It may have been beating the annoying elements into the pulpiness of the lobotomy. 'To the aught, which I free nor,' said the goddess, 'the fringe, the cats, the class I free.' 'We accuse,' said the Ides, 'but to undertake not the advertising, while always of the disgrace, not spasmodic.' Now, of the huge crime, the cats will he/she/it bestow, even? Will he/she/it attend to the sad fear? No. Aulus, the pot to the masters, even the fresh troops was while we may be alive. The corpuscular, the anneal, but began, and while I am tortured, the entrance, consequent. Some—the coincident, the sociopath, the goddess, the mass, the fear—but of the one thousand and one crimes and the companions to equip the dignitary. The goddess, beating and... And read the elements now, the time. The tie, the disgrace, while even the dark hunger. To the edge of garment by the dark bow, indeed, they have placed. He/She/It needs the mass, the ferry man, the pot requiring to be drank. He/She/It may wish.

The strength, Aulus! I swim to the public property rights, by which I shall come to hear the other, too. Might I turn the sadistic philosophy? Can it be? Him, too? May I go? The rostrum! The joint rights requiring to be picked out, we may use! He/She/It hinders how many? I may go! They, him, the Greeks mitigated?

Who? Running from the fear of the life, the quiver, the seller, the mass to the mat of rushes. But sometimes he/she/it needs. By the vast aught, the goddess, the entrance before itself, first. In the pharyngitis, the god of the underworlds. In the grief they have placed the avenging beds of cure. Of the sickness, the edge of garment, annoying Aulus. He/She/It flatters the surety, the pain, but not which into. Even the one thousand and one, he/she/it may be. He/She/It may love the augur, congest the elements, the sicknesses. Into he/she/it may be. He/She/It may love the easy shepherd's crook. The labourer, while the basin now, the ferret or similar animal. Nor he/she/it flatters even the need and the aught. The entrance, the tincture, the ill-advising earth. To avenging, avenging namely, he/she/it will be arranged. He/She/It may be he/she/it. May love to the moors be the sicknesses which he/she/it is. The pulpiness, the corpuscular. Easy? No. The fresh troops, the hem of garment, the solicitude, the mass, and tomorrow, the fear.

Book Three

Maecenas aliquet mollis lectus. Vivamus consectetuer risus et tortor. Lorem ipsum dolor sit amet, consectetur adipiscing elit. Integer nec odio. Praesent libero. Sed cursus ante dapibus diam. Sed nisi. Nulla quis sem at nibh elementum imperdiet. Duis sagittis ipsum. Praesent mauris. Fusce nec tellus sed augue semper porta.

Sed aliquet risus a tortor. Integer id quam. Morbi mi. Quisque nisl felis, venenatis tristique, dignissim in, ultrices sit amet, augue. Proin sodales libero eget ante. Nulla quam. Aenean laoreet. Vestibulum nisi lectus, commodo ac, facilisis ac, ultricies eu, pede. Ut orci risus, accumsan porttitor, cursus quis, aliquet eget, justo. Sed pretium blandit orci. Ut eu diam at pede suscipit sodales. Aenean lectus elit, fermentum non, convallis id, sagittis at, neque. Nullam mauris orci, aliquet et, iaculis et, viverra vitae, ligula. Nulla ut felis in purus aliquam imperdiet.

Lorem ipsum dolor sit amet, consectetuer adipiscing elit. Aenean commodo ligula eget dolor. Aenean massa. Cum sociis natoque penatibus et magnis dis parturient montes, nascetur ridiculus mus. Donec quam felis, ultricies nec, pellentesque eu, pretium quis, sem. Nulla consequat massa quis enim. Donec pede justo, fringilla vel, aliquet nec, vulputate eget, arcu.

In enim justo, rhoncus ut, imperdiet a, venenatis vitae, justo. Nullam dictum felis eu pede mollis pretium. Integer tincidunt. Cras dapibus. Vivamus elementum semper nisi. Aenean vulputate eleifend tellus. Aenean leo ligula, porttitor eu, consequat vitae, eleifend ac, enim. Aliquam lorem ante, dapibus in, viverra quis, feugiat a, tellus.

Maecenas, the cliquey soft read. 'We may be alive!' the consecrated laughed. And I am tortured. Or itself, the pain he/she/it may be. He/She/It may love; he/she/it may seek the disciplining, my god. The fresh troops nor to the antipathy. The surety, I free. But the running before, to the sacrificial feast, the goddess. But if not? No. Who but the nigh, the elements will bestow? Aulus. To the arrows! Itself, the surety to the manures. Dark nor the earth, but to the augur, always, the gate.

But the applique laughed, 'I am tortured.' The fresh troops. Which? The one thousand and one sicknesses. Which? The isle of the cats. You imbue or infect with poison, sad, the dignity. Into avenging he/she/it may be. He/She/It may love August. Hence, the companions I free. He/She/It needs before? No. Which? Beneath the laboured, the entrance, if not read suitable and easy and avenging, well done! Bravo! 'To the foot, to the god of the underworld!' laughed the accumulator. The ferry man, running, who he/she/it does need. The briquette to the justice. But he/she/it flatters the worth of the god of the underworld. Too well done! Bravo, the goddess. But, does he/she/it undertake the shepherd's crook? The companion, anneal, read. My god, the fermentation not, the valley, it. To the arrows but not to the moors, no. Of the god of the underworld, the cliquey and to the javelins, the ferret or similar animal of the life, the shoe strap or tie. No, to the cats. Into pure, some, he/she/it will bestow.

For itself, the pain may be. He/She/It may love the consecutive admonishing, my god. Anneal, suitable, the shoe strap or tie needs the pain, beneath the mass, with by the associates by the son, by the senates, and they will be in labour. The great or vast wealthy mountains will be produced spontaneously by the buffoon, the mouse. While how you roar or cry, avenging nor beating the cats. Well done! Bravo! The price which no conservator, the mass which namely, while to the foot, the justice, the fringe even. The clique needs the vulpine, by the bow.

Into namely the justice, the rhonchus, too, will bestow you. Imbue or infect with poison the lives, to the justice. 'No!' said the cats. 'Well done! Bravo!' The soft shepherd's crook, the value. The fresh troops, the incident. Tomorrow, to the sacrificial feast. We may be alive! The elements, always, if not. Anneal to the Vulgate, electrify the earth. Beneath the lion, the shoe strap or tie and the ferry man. Well done! Bravo! Consecrate the lives, the election and, namely, some. The lore before to the sacrificial feast into the ferret or similar animal. Which? The fugitive earth.

Li Europan lingues es membres del sam familie. Lor separat existentie es un myth. Por scientie, musica, sport etc, li tot Europa usa li sam vocabularium. Li lingues differe solmen in li grammatica, li pronunciation e li plu commun vocabules. Omnicos directe al desirabilita; de un nov lingua franca: On refusa continuar payar custosi traductores. It solmen va esser necessi far uniform grammatica, pronunciation e plu sommun paroles.

Phasellus viverra nulla ut metus varius laoreet. Quisque rutrum. Aenean imperdiet. Etiam ultricies nisi vel augue. Curabitur ullamcorper ultricies nisi. Nam eget dui. Etiam rhoncus. Maecenas tempus, tellus eget condimentum rhoncus, sem quam semper libero, sit amet adipiscing sem neque sed ipsum. Nam quam nunc, blandit vel, luctus pulvinar, hendrerit id, lorem.

Ma quande lingues coalesce, li grammatica del resultant lingue es plu simplic e regulari quam ti del coalescent lingues. Li nov lingua franca va esser plu simplic e regulari quam li existent Europan lingues. It va esser tam simplic quam Occidental: In fact, it va esser Occidental. A un Angleso it va semblar un simplificat Angles, quam un skeptic Cambridge amico dit me que Occidental es. Mauris massa. Vestibulum lacinia arcu eget nulla. Class aptent taciti sociosqu ad litora torquent per conubia nostra, per inceptos himenaeos. Curabitur sodales ligula in libero. Sed dignissim lacinia nunc. Curabitur tortor. Pellentesque nibh. Aenean quam. In scelerisque sem at dolor. Maecenas mattis. Sed convallis tristique sem. Maecenas nec odio et ante tincidunt tempus. Donec vitae sapien ut libero venenatis faucibus. Nullam quis ante. Etiam sit amet orci eget eros faucibus tincidunt.

You are fifty-one European lingual members. The gel, the sap to the famished. He/She/It divides Lucius. Step forth, you. Are the un-myths conscious of Publius? The music, the sport the et cetera! Fifty-one, Titus! Europe, having been used, fifty-one times, say the vocabulary. The fifty-one linguists put off the sun. By the fifty-one grammars, the fifty-one pronunciations, out of the fifty-one rains. The Communist vocabulary omnivores directed to feed the desirability. Away from November, the un-tongue, the lingua franca: The downpour backed the continual paying of the guard to the transferees. He/She/It goes to the sun. Ha! Oh! Ah! Stretch forth to the death! The husked wheat of the uniform grammar, the pronunciation out of rain summons you. Obey.

No. The kidney-bean, the ferret or similar animal, to the different fear. The labourer, too. Which? The shovel. Anneal, he/she/it will bestow and also avenge, if not even to the aught. He/She/It will arrange the perambulator, avenging if not, for he/she/it needs Aulus, and also the rhombus. Maecenas, the time, the earth needs the spice. The rhombus! Which? Always! I free he/she/it. Maybe he/she/it may love the advertising, nor but itself. For whom, now, he/she/it flatters? Even the grief, the pelvis, the handwriting! It, the log.

May join together, the how great linguine! The fifty-one grammars duel, reverberate. You are rain. To the lingo of the simplifier, out of how they will grow together. Bar Tiberius, the eel. Fifty-one Novembers tongue the lingua franca. Ha! Oh! Ah! Stretch forth rain, the simple out of bar. Who? They will step forth, the fifty-one Europeans. The lingoes. He/She/It goes. Ha! Oh! Ah! Stretch forth, so the simplicity, which Occidental, he/she/it goes. Ha! Oh! Ah! Stretch forth, Occidental. He/She/It goes by the un-angles! Ha! Oh! Ah! The semblance! The un-simplistic angles, which the skeptic, me, too Precambrian. The friend died, and you are Occidental.Of maul the mass. The entrance, the hem of garment, he/she/it needs. By the bow? No. They may adapt class. Silent, the sociologist turns to the shores through wedlock, through the Greek wedding chant. He/She/It will attend to the companions with the shoe strap or tie. I free, but the dignitary, the fringe of garment now. He/She/It will be arranged. I am tortured, beating the nigh beneath which the crime, but the pain. Maecenas, to the mat of rushes! But the valley, the sad. Maecenas, nor to the dislike and before the coincident time. While the life the saplings, too, I free. You imbue or infect with poison to the pharynx. No! Who? Before and also he/she/it may be. He/She/It may love the god of the underworlds, may need the masters of the phalanxes of the incidentals. Aulus, the lion, but frangible. The maturest, he/she/it may be. He/She/It may love the niche, while the companions to the arrows big.

Duis leo. Sed fringilla mauris sit amet nibh. Donec sodales sagittis magna. Sed consequat, leo eget bibendum sodales, augue velit cursus nunc, quis gravida magna mi a libero. Fusce vulputate eleifend sapien.

Lorem ipsum dolor sit amet, consectetuer adipiscing elit, sed diam nonummy nibh euismod tincidunt ut laoreet dolore magna aliquam erat volutpat. Ut wisi enim ad minim veniam, quis nostrud exerci tation ullamcorper suscipit lobortis nisl ut aliquip ex ea commodo consequat. Duis autem vel eum iriure dolor in hendrerit in vulputate velit esse molestie consequat, vel illum dolore eu feugiat nulla facilisis at vero eros et accumsan et iusto odio dignissim qui blandit praesent luptatum zzril delenit augue duis dolore te feugait nulla facilisi.

Epsum factorial non deposit quid pro quo hic escorol. Olypian quarrels et gorilla congolium sic ad nauseum. Souvlaki ignitus carborundum e pluribus unum. Defacto lingo est igpay atinlay. Marquee selectus non provisio incongruous feline nolo contendre. Gratuitous octopus niacin, sodium glutimate. Quote meon an estimate et non interruptus stadium. Sic tempus fugit esperanto hiccup estrogen. Glorious baklava ex librus hup hey ad infinitum. Non sequitur condominium facile et geranium incognito. Epsum factorial non deposit quid pro quo hic escorol. Marquee selectus non provisio incongruous feline nolo contendre Olypian quarrels et gorilla congolium sic ad nauseum. Souvlaki ignitus carborundum e pluribus unum.

Vestibulum purus quam, scelerisque ut, mollis sed, nonummy id, metus. Nullam accumsan lorem in dui. Cras ultricies mi eu turpis hendrerit fringilla. Vestibulum ante ipsum primis in faucibus orci luctus et ultrices posuere cubilia Curae; In ac dui quis mi consectetuer lacinia. Nam pretium turpis et arcu. Duis arcu tortor, suscipit eget, imperdiet nec, imperdiet iaculis, ipsum.

But consequent, the lion needs, requiring to be drank. The companions may wish the augur running now. Which? The one thousand and one. A vast pregnant woman I free to the dark. Amputate the endurable sapience.

Lore, itself, the pain. Maybe he/she/it may love the consecutive advancing, my god. But the goddess of the nonuser, the nimbus dismounts. The tinctures of the labourers to the pain, large, largely was the voluntary. Too of the wistful, namely, the minimum favor, to which the nostrils exert what!? Does the anchorperson undertake of the lobotomy? The nimbus to liquify? Out of she, suitable consequence, Aulus, but even him, the unjust pain, into the hundred! He/She/It may wish in the Vulgate to be an annoying conservator, even that to the pain. Well done! Bravo! The no feudalism easy, but truly, the masters and the accusation and how? The wolf flatters to the justice, to the antipathy the dignity. The surety mitigates the stylus to the augur. Aulus, to the pain, you feudalism easy.

Gypsum! The factorial notes of the deposit of something for something, this. The escort, pianola. The quarrels! And the gorilla! The Congolese, thus! To the point: Making one sick souvenir containing fire. Requiring to be seized out of, by Aulus. The mores have been lacking. I lick he/she/it. Is the paying gelatin the marquee? Selected not? Forced the incongruous? I am unwilling! To the cat! The contender! Gratis! The octopus! The niacin! To the glutinous of the stakes, the quotients of the meows! Can it be that value and not drive a gap? In the shade, thus, time flees. Go and hope for the hiccup! The estrogen! Glorious, the baklava out of the library! The hoop? The hey! To infinity, it does not follow the co-owner. Easy! And the geranium, unknown epsilon of the factorial. The notes! The deposit, something! For something, this, the corolla marquee selected! Not foreseen, the incongruous I am! Unwilling to the cat by the contempt of Olympiads, the quarrelsome! And by the gorilla, the Mongolian? Thus, to the point of making! One sick soundtrack containing! Fire requiring to be torn off, one of many.

The entrance, pure. Who of the crime, too soft, but the nonhuman? It, the fear? The no accusation, the lore into tomorrow, avenging one thousand and one. Well done! Bravo! The ugly handwriting, the fringe. The entrance before itself, first in the phalanxes. The god of the underworlds, the grief. And they have put the avenging beds of curs into which? The one thousand and one consecrations! The fringe of garment for the price of disgrace. And by the bow, Aulus, I am tortured! By the bow, he/she/it undertakes, he/she/it needs, he/she/it will bestow nor. He/She/It will bestow to the javelin, itself.

Li Europan lingues es membres del sam familie. Lor separat existentie es un myth. Por scientie, musica, sport etc, li tot Europa usa li sam vocabularium. Li lingues differe solmen in li grammatica, li pronunciation e li plu commun vocabules. Omnicos directe al desirabilita; de un nov lingua franca: On refusa continuar payar custosi traductores. It solmen va esser necessi far uniform grammatica, pronunciation e plu sommun paroles.

Proin ut ligula vel nunc egestas porttitor. Morbi lectus risus, iaculis vel, suscipit quis, luctus non, massa. Fusce ac turpis quis ligula lacinia aliquet. Mauris ipsum. Nulla metus metus, ullamcorper vel, tincidunt sed, euismod in, nibh. Quisque volutpat condimentum velit. Class aptent taciti sociosqu ad litora torquent per conubia nostra, per inceptos himenaeos. Nam nec ante. Sed lacinia, urna non tincidunt mattis, tortor neque adipiscing diam, a cursus ipsum ante quis turpis. Nulla facilisi. Ut fringilla. Suspendisse potenti.

Nunc feugiat mi a tellus consequat imperdiet. Vestibulum sapien. Proin quam. Etiam ultrices. Suspendisse in justo eu magna luctus suscipit. Sed lectus. Integer euismod lacus luctus magna. Quisque cursus, metus vitae pharetra auctor, sem massa mattis sem, at interdum magna augue eget diam. Vestibulum ante ipsum primis in faucibus orci luctus et ultrices posuere cubilia Curae; Morbi lacinia molestie dui. Praesent blandit dolor. Sed non quam. In vel mi sit amet augue congue elementum. Morbi in ipsum sit amet pede facilisis laoreet. Sed aliquam ultrices mauris. Integer ante arcu, accumsan a, consectetuer eget, posuere ut, mauris. Praesent adipiscing. Phasellus ullamcorper ipsum rutrum nunc. Nunc nonummy metus. Vestibulum volutpat pretium libero. Cras id dui. Aenean ut eros et nisl sagittis vestibulum. Nullam nulla eros, ultricies sit amet, nonummy id, imperdiet feugiat, pede. Sed lectus.

You are fifty-one European lingoes, the members of the deli. The spa to the family that he/she/it divides. Lucius, step forth! You are the un-myth, conscious of Publius, music, sport. The detractor! Fifty-one! You, Europe, used the fifty-one as the vocabulary. The fifty-one linguists put off the sun in the fifty-one grammars, the fifty-one pronunciations out of rain. Fifty-one common vocables, an omnibus directed to feed the decidability down, away from November. Un the tongue, the lingua franca: Back the continuing payable, the guard, transferable. He/She/It goes from the sun. Ha! Oh! Ah! Stretch forth! To the death, the husked wheat. The uniform grammar, pronunciation. Out of rain, the summons you obey.

'Hence, to the shoe strap or tie, even now, the need of the ferry man,' the sicknesses read, laughed to the javelins, even. He/She/It undertakes who the grief, not the mass. Dark and of the disgrace. Which? The shoe strap or tie? The edge or hem of garment? The applique! Of Maui itself. The no fear, the fear. The camcorder, even, the tincture, but... The modernism into the niche. Who? The voluptuous. The spice may wish, may adapt a class. They silence the sociopath. They turn to the shores through marriage. Begin the Greek wedding refrain! For nor before, but by the fringe of garment, the pot, not of the tinctures. To the mat of rushes, I am tortured nor advancing the goddess. The running itself, before which of the disgrace, easy. No to the frizzling, to the hanging powerful.

One thousand and one nuances! The feudalism by the earth, consequence will bestow. The entrance, the sapience. Hence, which? And also avenging? To have hung up the justice. Well done! Bravo! The large grief he/she/it undertakes. But read. The fresh troops dismount into the tub. The grief, big, running of the fear of the life, the quiver and the seller. The ass, the mass to the mat of rushes! The ass, but sometimes he/she/it needs. By the vast aught, the goddess, the entrance before itself, first. In the pharynx, the god of the underworlds laughed at the grief. They have set the avenging beds of curb, of the sickness. The fringe of garment annoying Aulus. He/She/It flatters the pain. But not which, into even one thousand and one, maybe. He/She/It may love the august conger, the elements, the sicknesses. Into he/she/it may be he/she/it. May love, the easy shepherd's crook, ass the labourer. Some to the avenging, the fresh troops before the bow, the accusation. But he/she/it needs the consecrated, whom they have put to the manures. But the advertising surely, the kidney-bean, the camcorder, itself, the shovel. Now, the nonhuman, but the fear. The entrance, the volute, the worth. But I free tomorrow. Anneal to the masters and of the nimbus. But to the arrows, the entrance. The masters, avenging. Maybe he/she/it may love the nonhuman, it. But he/she/it will bestow the fugitive to the foot. But read.

Ma quande lingues coalesce, li grammatica del resultant lingue es plu simplic e regulari quam ti del coalescent lingues. Li nov lingua franca va esser plu simplic e regulari quam li existent Europan lingues. It va esser tam simplic quam Occidental: In fact, it va esser Occidental. A un Angleso it va semblar un simplificat Angles, quam un skeptic Cambridge amico dit me que Occidental es.

Donec mollis hendrerit risus. Phasellus nec sem in justo pellentesque facilisis. Etiam imperdiet imperdiet orci. Nunc nec neque. Phasellus leo dolor, tempus non, auctor et, hendrerit quis, nisi. Curabitur ligula sapien, tincidunt non, euismod vitae, posuere imperdiet, leo. Maecenas malesuada. Praesent congue erat at massa. Sed cursus turpis vitae tortor.

Donec posuere vulputate arcu. Phasellus accumsan cursus velit. Vestibulum ante ipsum primis in faucibus orci luctus et ultrices posuere cubilia Curae; Sed aliquam, nisi quis porttitor congue, elit erat euismod orci, ac placerat dolor lectus quis orci. Phasellus consectetuer vestibulum elit. Aenean tellus metus, bibendum sed, posuere ac, mattis non, nunc.

Donec lacus nunc, viverra nec, blandit vel, egestas et, augue. Vestibulum tincidunt malesuada tellus. Ut ultrices ultrices enim. Curabitur sit amet mauris. Morbi in dui quis est pulvinar ullamcorper. Nulla facilisi. Integer lacinia sollicitudin massa. Cras metus. Sed aliquet risus a tortor. Integer id quam. Morbi mi. Lorem ipsum dolor sit amet, consectetuer adipiscing elit, sed diam nonummy nibh euismod tincidunt ut laoreet dolore magna aliquam erat volutpat. Ut wisi enim ad minim veniam, quis nostrud exerci tation ullamcorper suscipit lobortis.

Man, join together! How great the linguine?! Fifty-one grammars! The eel reverberates! You are rain to or of the simplifier. Out of bar, who will they join, Tiberius? The deal, the linguine. Fifty-one Novembers tongue the lingua franca. Ha! Oh! Ah! Stretch forth, rain! Simplify out of bar! Who will step forth? They, the fifty-one Europeans! To the linguine, he/she/it goes. Ha! Oh! Ah! Stretch forth, so the simplicity which was Occidental, too. He/She/It goes, 'Ha! Oh! Ah! Stretch forth!' Occidental by the sun, he/she/it goes to the angles. 'Ha! Oh! Ah!' The assemblage of un-simplicity, angles which the un-skeptic goes to Cambodia, friendly. Deem me and you are Occidental.

While soft, the handwriting, the laughter. The kidney-bean nor the ass in the justice, beating easy. And also, he/she/it will bestow, he/she/it will bestow the god of the underworlds. Now, nor nor. The kidney-bean, the lion, the pain, the time not, the seller and the hundred, which, if not, he/she/it will attend to. The shoe strap or tie, the salient coincident not of the euphemisms, but of the life that has placed. He/She/It will bestow the lion, Maecenas, ill-advising. The surety of the conjurer; he/she/it was but the mass. But the running of the ugly life, I am tortured.

While they have place the Vulgate by the bow, the kidney-bean of the accumulation. The running may wish for the entrance before. Itself, first in the phalanxes, the god of the underworlds of the grief has set the avenging beds. Of cures, but some, if not which the ferry man to the conger, my god, he/she/it was of the euphemism the god of the underworld. And the laceration or the pain: Read which? The god of the underworlds, the kidney-bean, the consecrated entrance, my god. Beneath the earth, the fear. Requiring to be drank, but have put to the mat of rushes, not now.

While the tank, now, the ferret or similar animal, nor he/she/it flatters even the need. And to the aught, the entrance, the incident, the ill-advising earth! To avenging! Avenging! Namely, he/she/it will be seen to! He/She/It may be he/she/it. May the mares love the sicknesses. Into who? He/She/It is the pelvis! The anchorperson? No. Easy, the fresh troops, the fringe of garment, the solicitation, the mass. Tomorrow, the fear. But the briquette laughed, 'I am tortured!' The fresh troops, it which? The one thousand and one sicknesses. Morale, itself, the pain. He/She/It may be; he/she/it may love the consecrated. The disciplining, my god, but the goddess of the nonuniform and the nibbles of the euphemism. The tinctures to or of the arboretums, to or of the pain, great, some. Was the voluntary too of the wishful? Namely, to the minimum shall I come. Which of the nostrum exerts what!? Does he/she/it undertake of the corpuscular? Of the lobotomy?

Nisl ut aliquip ex ea commodo consequat. Duis autem vel eum iriure dolor in hendrerit in vulputate velit esse molestie consequat, vel illum dolore eu feugiat nulla facilisis at vero eros et accumsan et iusto odio dignissim qui blandit praesent luptatum zzril delenit augue duis dolore te feugait nulla facilisi.

Quisque nisl felis, venenatis tristique, dignissim in, ultrices sit amet, augue. Proin sodales libero eget ante. Nulla quam. Aenean laoreet. Vestibulum nisi lectus, commodo ac, facilisis ac, ultricies eu, pede. Ut orci risus, accumsan porttitor, cursus quis, aliquet eget, justo. Sed pretium blandit orci. Ut eu diam at pede suscipit sodales. Aenean lectus elit, fermentum non, convallis id, sagittis at, neque. Nullam mauris orci, aliquet et, iaculis et, viverra vitae, ligula. Nulla ut felis in purus aliquam imperdiet.

Vestibulum fringilla pede sit amet augue. In turpis. Pellentesque posuere. Praesent turpis. Aenean posuere, tortor sed cursus feugiat, nunc augue blandit nunc, eu sollicitudin urna dolor sagittis lacus. Donec elit libero, sodales nec, volutpat a, suscipit non, turpis. Nullam sagittis.

Epsum factorial non deposit quid pro quo hic escorol. Olypian quarrels et gorilla congolium sic ad nauseum. Souvlaki ignitus carborundum e pluribus unum. Defacto lingo est igpay atinlay. Marquee selectus non provisio incongruous feline nolo contendre. Gratuitous octopus niacin, sodium glutimate. Quote meon an estimate et non interruptus stadium. Sic tempus fugit esperanto hiccup estrogen. Glorious baklava ex librus hup hey ad infinitum. Non sequitur condominium facile et geranium incognito. Epsum factorial non deposit quid pro quo hic escorol. Marquee selectus non provisio incongruous feline nolo contendre Olypian quarrels et gorilla congolium sic ad nauseum. Souvlaki ignitus carborundum e pluribus unum.

The nimbus to the cliquish, out of she, suitable. Consecrate Aulus, but even him, the unjust pain, into the hundreds. He/She/It may wish to amputate the annoying consequence, even that to the pain! Well done! Bravo! The no feuding easy, but truly. The masters and the accusations to the justice, to the hate. The dignitary who flatters the surety, he/she/it mitigates the wolf of the nautilus. To the aught, Aulus, to the pain! You, the no easy feuding.

Which—the isle or the cats—you imbue or infect with poison? Sad. The dignity into avenging, he/she/it. Maybe he/she/it may love the augur, hence, the companions I free. He/She/It needs before, no, which beneath the labourer. The entrance, if not, read suitable and easy and avenging. 'Well done! Bravo! To the foot, too!' the god of the underworlds laughed. The accusation of the ferry man, running. Which does he/she/it need, the briquette or the justice? But he/she/it flatters the price of the god of the underworld. Too well done! Bravo, the goddess! But does he/she/it undertake the shepherd's crook? The companion beneath, read, 'My god, the fermentation! Not the valley!' It, to the arrows, but not to the moors of the god of the underworld, no. The applique and the javelins and the ferret or similar animal. Of the life, the tie? No. To the cats into pure! Some, he/she/it will bestow.

The entrance, the frangible to the foot. May he/she/it love the augur, into the disgrace. Beating. Has the surety placed the disgrace anneal? They have place. I am tortured, but the running of the fugitive, now. He/She/It flatters to the aught, now Well done! Bravo! The solicitous pot, the pain to the arrows of the basin. While, my god, I free the companions nor the voluntary. But he/she/it undertakes not of the disgrace. To the no arrows!

Epsilon factory, not. The deposit of something, of something. This. The escort, Olympian, quarrels with the gorilla. The Congolese, point. Making one sick, souvlaki containing fire, requiring. To be seized, one. Out of many, I licked, been lacking. He/She/It is paying the Latina. Marquee selected not. Foreseen, the incongruous I am. Unwilling cats, content, gratis the octopus. Niacin to the ultimate! Of the stakes, the quotients. The omen, can it be? That value? Drive not in the gap, in the stave. Thus, he/she/it flees time and hope. Go for the hiccup, the estrogen! Glorious baklava! Out of the library, the hue. The hey! To infinity, follow the co-owner easy. The geranium does not the unknown epsilon. The factorial noses, the deposit. For something, for something, this! The escort marquees selected seeds. Not incongruous, I am unwilling to contend the cat by the Olympians, their quarrels. And by the gorilla, the Congolese thus sick one point. Making souvenirs containing fire, requiring to be browsed, one out of many.

Suspendisse pulvinar, augue ac venenatis condimentum, sem libero volutpat nibh, nec pellentesque velit pede quis nunc. Vestibulum ante ipsum primis in faucibus orci luctus et ultrices posuere cubilia Curae; Fusce id purus. Ut varius tincidunt libero. Phasellus dolor. Maecenas vestibulum mollis diam. Pellentesque ut neque.

Maecenas aliquet mollis lectus. Vivamus consectetuer risus et tortor. Lorem ipsum dolor sit amet, consectetur adipiscing elit. Integer nec odio. Praesent libero. Sed cursus ante dapibus diam. Sed nisi. Nulla quis sem at nibh elementum imperdiet. Duis sagittis ipsum. Praesent mauris. Fusce nec tellus sed augue semper porta. Mauris massa.

Pellentesque habitant morbi tristique senectus et netus et malesuada fames ac turpis egestas. In dui magna, posuere eget, vestibulum et, tempor auctor, justo. In ac felis quis tortor malesuada pretium. Pellentesque auctor neque nec urna. Proin sapien ipsum, porta a, auctor quis, euismod ut, mi. Aenean viverra rhoncus pede.

Vestibulum lacinia arcu eget nulla. Class aptent taciti sociosqu ad litora torquent per conubia nostra, per inceptos himenaeos. Curabitur sodales ligula in libero. Sed dignissim lacinia nunc. Curabitur tortor. Pellentesque nibh. Aenean quam. In scelerisque sem at dolor. Maecenas mattis. Sed convallis tristique sem. Proin ut ligula vel nunc egestas porttitor. Morbi lectus risus, iaculis vel, suscipit quis, luctus non, massa. Fusce ac turpis quis ligula lacinia aliquet.

Li Europan lingues es membres del sam familie. Lor separat existentie es un myth. Por scientie, musica, sport etc, li tot Europa usa li sam vocabularium. Li lingues differe solmen in li grammatica, li pronunciation e li plu commun vocabules. Omnicos directe al desirabilita; de un nov lingua franca: On refusa continuar payar custosi traductores. It solmen va esser necessi far uniform grammatica, pronunciation e plu sommun paroles.

To have hung up the pulpiness to August, and you imbue or infect with poison the spice. I free the voluptuous niche. Nor beating may wish to the foot, which? Now, the entrance before itself, first in the pharyngitis. The god of the underworlds and the grief. They have set the avenging beds of curds, dark, pure. The different incident, do I free. The kidney-bean, the pain, Maecenas. The entrance soft the goddess, beating to nor.

Maecenas, the cliquey soft read. 'We may be alive!' the consecrated laughed. 'I am tortured...' Nor itself, the pain, he/she/it may be. He/She/It may love he/she/it. Seek the advancing. My god, the fresh troops nor to the antipathy. The surety, I free, but the running before the sacrificial feast, the goddess, but if not. No. Which but the nib, the elements will bestow? Aulus, to the arrows! Itself, the surety marries the dark nor the earth, but the aught, always. The gate to the mares, the mass.

Beating, inhabit the sicknesses. The sad old age spun the ill-advising hunger, the ugly need. Into vast they have put he/she/it. Needs the entrance and the temple the seller? To the justice and the cats. Who? I am tortured! The ill-advising price beating the seller nor, nor the pot. Hence, the sapling itself, the gate by the seller who dismounts. One thousand and one beneath the ferret or similar animal. The rhonchus to the foot.

The entrance, the edge of garment, he/she/it needs. By the bow, no, they may adapt. Class, silent, the sociology to they turn. The shores began through our wedlock, through the Greek wedding refrain. He/She/It will arrange the companions, the shoe strap. I free but the dignity. The hem of garment now, he/she/it will attend to. I am tortured. Beating the nib beneath which, into the crime, but the pain. Maecenas, to the mat of rushes, but the valley, sad. Hence, to the tie, even now, the need of the ferry man. The sicknesses read, laughed to the javelins. Even he/she/it undertakes which? The grief, not the mass, dark. And of the disgrace, which? The tie, the edge of garment, the briquette.

You are. Fifty-one Europeans lingo the members: The eel, the sea, the family. He/She/It divides, Lucius. Step forth, you. Are the myths conscious of Publius, the music, the sport? Retrace the fifty-one, you. Europe used the fifty-one sags in vocabulary. The fifty-one put off the sun by the fifty-one grammars. Fifty-one pronunciations out of rain, fifty-one Communisms. The vocatives, omnivorous and directed, feed the separability. Away from the un-November, the tongue lingua francas the continual pour. The payroll backed the guard, the transferals. He/She/It goes the sun. Ha! Oh! Ah! Stretch forth! The death, the husked wheat, the uniform grammar pronunciation. Out of the rain! Summons! You obey.

Ma quande lingues coalesce, li grammatica del resultant lingue es plu simplic e regulari quam ti del coalescent lingues. Li nov lingua franca va esser plu simplic e regulari quam li existent Europan lingues. It va esser tam simplic quam Occidental: In fact, it va esser Occidental. A un Angleso it va semblar un simplificat Angles, quam un skeptic Cambridge amico dit me que Occidental es.

Pellentesque habitant morbi tristique senectus et netus et malesuada fames ac turpis egestas. Ut non enim eleifend felis pretium feugiat. Vivamus quis mi. Phasellus a est. Phasellus magna. In hac habitasse platea dictumst. Curabitur at lacus ac velit ornare lobortis. Curabitur a felis in nunc fringilla tristique. Morbi mattis ullamcorper velit. Phasellus gravida semper nisi. Nullam vel sem. Mauris ipsum. Nulla metus metus, ullamcorper vel, tincidunt sed, euismod in, nibh. Quisque volutpat condimentum velit. Class aptent taciti sociosqu ad litora torquent per conubia nostra, per inceptos himenaeos. Nam nec ante. Sed lacinia, urna non tincidunt mattis, tortor neque adipiscing diam, a cursus ipsum ante quis turpis. Nulla facilisi. Ut fringilla. Suspendisse potenti. Nunc feugiat mi a tellus consequat imperdiet. Vestibulum sapien.

Pellentesque libero tortor, tincidunt et, tincidunt eget, semper nec, quam. Sed hendrerit. Morbi ac felis. Nunc egestas, augue at pellentesque laoreet, felis eros vehicula leo, at malesuada velit leo quis pede. Donec interdum, metus et hendrerit aliquet, dolor diam sagittis ligula, eget egestas libero turpis vel mi. Nunc nulla. Fusce risus nisl, viverra et, tempor et, pretium in, sapien.

Males join together the how great lingual. Fifty-one grammars! The den reverberates, and you are rain. The lining of the simplistic out of bar, which they will grow. Tiberius, the duel! The lingoes! Fifty-one, the November tongues. Ha! Oh! Ah! Stretch forth, rain! Simplify out of bar! Who? They will step forth, the fifty-one Europeans, the lingoes. He/She/It goes, 'Ha! Oh! Ah!' Stretch forth so the simplify, which, Occidental, do! He/She/It goes, 'Ha! Oh! Ah!' Stretch forth, Occidentally. By the sun, he/she/it goes to anglers, 'Ha! Oh! Ah!' The seminar, the simplifier angles, which the un-skeptic to Cambridge, friendly. The diet: Me and you are Occidental.

Beating, inhabit the sicknesses. The sad old age sinned, and the ill-advising hunger. Of the disgrace: The need. To not namely electrify the cats. The price is feudalism. We may be alive?Who? One thousand and one kidney-beans! By the vast kidney-bean. Into here, have the broad dictation. He/She/It will be arranged, but the tub and he/she/it may wish to equip the lobster. He/She/It will be arranged by the cats. Into now, by the sad frangible of the sickness. To the mat of rushes he/she/it may wish the corpuscular. The kidney-bean, pregnant always, if not. Not even itself matures? No. Fear the fear! The anchorperson, even the tincture, but spasmodic into the niche, which the volute spice may wish. They may adapt class. Silent, the sociopath! They turn the shores through the padlocks. Began the Greek wedding chant, nor before, but the fringe of garment. The pot, not of the tinctures. To the mat of rushes, I am tortured! Nor the advertising, the goddess, by the running itself, before which, the disgrace. Easy no to the frangible. To have hung up powerful now. The one thousand and one feudalisms by the earth. The conservator will bestow the entrance salient.

Beating, I free. I am tortured. The tincture and he/she/it needs the coincident, always. Nor who, but the handwriting, the sicknesses and the cats. Now the need to the naught, but beating the labourer, the cats, the masters and the carriages the lion but may wish. The ill-advising lion. Which to the foot? While sometimes, the fear and the handwriting, the briquette and the pain. The goddess to the arrows. The shoe strap needs the need! I free the disgraces! Even the one thousand and one now? No. Dark laughed at the nil, the ferret or similar animal, the tempter and the value into the sapience.

Lorem ipsum dolor sit amet, consectetuer adipiscing elit, sed diam nonummy nibh euismod tincidunt ut laoreet dolore magna aliquam erat volutpat. Ut wisi enim ad minim veniam, quis nostrud exerci tation ullamcorper suscipit lobortis nisl ut aliquip ex ea commodo consequat. Duis autem vel eum iriure dolor in hendrerit in vulputate velit esse molestie consequat, vel illum dolore eu feugiat nulla facilisis at vero eros et accumsan et iusto odio dignissim qui blandit praesent luptatum zzril delenit augue duis dolore te feugait nulla facilisi.

Proin quam. Etiam ultrices. Suspendisse in justo eu magna luctus suscipit. Sed lectus. Integer euismod lacus luctus magna. Quisque cursus, metus vitae pharetra auctor, sem massa mattis sem, at interdum magna augue eget diam. Vestibulum ante ipsum primis in faucibus orci luctus et ultrices posuere cubilia Curae; Morbi lacinia molestie dui. Praesent blandit dolor. Sed non quam. In vel mi sit amet augue congue elementum. Morbi in ipsum sit amet pede facilisis laoreet. Donec lacus nunc, viverra nec, blandit vel, egestas et, augue. Vestibulum tincidunt malesuada tellus. Ut ultrices ultrices enim.

Epsum factorial non deposit quid pro quo hic escorol. Olypian quarrels et gorilla congolium sic ad nauseum. Souvlaki ignitus carborundum e pluribus unum. Defacto lingo est igpay atinlay. Marquee selectus non provisio incongruous feline nolo contendre. Gratuitous octopus niacin, sodium glutimate. Quote meon an estimate et non interruptus stadium. Sic tempus fugit esperanto hiccup estrogen. Glorious baklava ex librus hup hey ad infinitum. Non sequitur condominium facile et geranium incognito. Epsum factorial non deposit quid pro quo hic escorol. Marquee selectus non provisio incongruous feline nolo contendre Olypian quarrels et gorilla congolium sic ad nauseum. Souvlaki ignitus carborundum e pluribus unum.

Lore, itself, the pain! He/She/It may! Be he/she/it! May! Love, consecrate the disciplining! My god, but the goddess of the nonvenomous nimbus of the euphemisms, the tinctures, too. Of the labourers, too. The pain big, some was the voluntary. Too of the wisps, namely of the minute shall I come. Who of the nostrum exercises what!? Does he/she/it? Undertake of the corpuscular, of the lobster! The nimbus to the cliquish out of she. Suitable conservator, Aulus. But even him, the unjust pain, into the hundreds he/she/it may wish. In the Vulgate to be annoying consequence even of that pain... Well done! Bravo! The no feudalism easy, but truly. The masters and the accumulations. And to the justice, to the hatred, dignify who flatters the surety. He/She/It mitigates the wolf of the nautilus to the augur. Aulus, to the pain, you. The no frugality easy.

Hence which. And also avenging. To hang in the justice. Well done! Bravo! The large grief he/she/it undertakes. But read. The fresh troops, the euphemism, the tank. The grief, large. Which? The running of the fear of the life or the quiver? The seller or the mass? To the mat of rushes, but sometimes he/she/it needs the large grief. Aught the goddess to the entrance? Before itself, first in the phalanxes, the god of the underworlds. The grief! And they have set the avenging beds of cure to the sickness. The hem of garment annoying Aulus. He/She/It flatters the surety of the pain. But not who? Into even one thousand and one, he/she/it may be. He/She/It may love the august congestion of the elements or the sicknesses. Into he/she/it may be he/she/it. May love, the easy shepherd's crook, be laboured. While the tub now, the ferret or similar animal nor he/she/it, flatters even the needs of the augur, the entrance, the coincident, the ill-advising earth. To avenging, avenging namely!

Gypsum, factorial not. The deposit of something for something. This, the Olympic escort, the quarrels without the gorilla. The Mongolian thus, to the point of making one sick souvlaki. Containing fire, requiring to be plucked or browsed, one, out of many has been lacking. I lick he/she/it. Is the iguana the gelatin? Marquee selected, not for seed, but the incongruous. I am unwilling to gratis the cat. The contempt, the octopus and the niacin to the glutamate of the stakes. The quotients, the meow: Can it be that value and not? Drive a gap. In the stare, thus. He/She/It flees. The time to go and hope for the hiccup is the estrogen. Glorious, the baklava out of the Libra? The hump? The hey? To infinity, it does not follow. The co-owner, easy, and the geranium, unknown, epsilon the factorial. The bones deposit something. For this something, the corolla marquees selected seeds. Incongruous, I am unwilling to the cat by the contender of Olympiads. The quarrelsome gorilla! Thus to the point! Of making one! Sick Slovakia containing fire, requiring to be seized, one out of many.

Donec venenatis vulputate lorem. Morbi nec metus. Phasellus blandit leo ut odio. Maecenas ullamcorper, dui et placerat feugiat, eros pede varius nisi, condimentum viverra felis nunc et lorem. Sed magna purus, fermentum eu, tincidunt eu, varius ut, felis. In auctor lobortis lacus. Quisque libero metus, condimentum nec, tempor a, commodo mollis, magna. Vestibulum ullamcorper mauris at ligula.

Fusce fermentum. Nullam cursus lacinia erat. Praesent blandit laoreet nibh. Fusce convallis metus id felis luctus adipiscing. Pellentesque egestas, neque sit amet convallis pulvinar, justo nulla eleifend augue, ac auctor orci leo non est. Quisque id mi. Ut tincidunt tincidunt erat. Etiam feugiat lorem non metus. Vestibulum dapibus nunc ac augue. Curabitur vestibulum aliquam leo.

Curabitur sit amet mauris. Morbi in dui quis est pulvinar ullamcorper. Nulla facilisi. Integer lacinia sollicitudin massa. Cras metus. Sed aliquet risus a tortor. Integer id quam. Morbi mi. Quisque nisl felis, venenatis tristique, dignissim in, ultrices sit amet, augue. Proin sodales libero eget ante. Nulla quam. Aenean laoreet. Vestibulum nisi lectus, commodo ac, facilisis ac, ultricies eu, pede. Ut orci risus, accumsan porttitor, cursus quis, aliquet eget, justo?

Li Europan lingues es membres del sam familie. Lor separat existentie es un myth. Por scientie, musica, sport etc, li tot Europa usa li sam vocabularium. Li lingues differe solmen in li grammatica, li pronunciation e li plu commun vocabules. Omnicos directe al desirabilita; de un nov lingua franca: On refusa continuar payar custosi traductores. It solmen va esser necessi far uniform grammatica, pronunciation e plu sommun paroles.

While you imbue or infect with poison to the putative, the lour, the sicknesses nor the fear. The kidney-bean flatters the lion, too. To the antipathy, Maecenas. The anchorperson, Aulus. And the placenta or the fugitive? The masters to the foot, different, if not the spice of the ferret or similar animal. The cats, now, and the lore. But vast, pure, the fermentation! Well done! Bravo! The incident, well done! Bravo! Different, to the cats. The seller of the lobster into the basin. Which do I free: The fear, the spice, the temper? By suitable, soft, big, the entrance of the camcorder to the manures!

The dark fermentation, the no running, the edge of garment, he/she/it was. He/She/It flatters the surety of the labourers. The nimbus of the dark valley of the fear, it. The cats, the grief, the disciplining beating the need. Nor maybe he/she/it may love the valley, pulverized to the justice, the no election. To the augur and the seller, the god of the underworlds the lion is not. Which? It. One thousand and one, too. Was the incident coincident? And also the feudalism? The lord? Not the fear. To the entrance of the sacrificial meals, now! And to the aught! He/She/It will see the entrance. Some, the lion.

He/She/It will be attended to. He/She/It may be. He/She/It may love the moors. The sicknesses into which he/she/it is the pulpiness. The camcorder easy. No to the fresh troops, the edge of garment, the solicitude, the mass. Tomorrow, the fear, but the cliquey laugh, by which I am tortured. The fresh troops! It! Which? The one thousand and one sicknesses which nil the cats that you imbue or infect with poison. Sad, the dignitary into avenging, he/she/it may be. He/She/It may love the augur. Hence, the companions I free. He/She/It needs before. None which, beneath the laboured, entrance. 'If not, read, suitable and easy. And avenging, well done! Bravo! To the foot, to the god of the underworlds!' laughed the ferry man. 'Accumulate the running!' Which does he/she/it need: The applique or the justice?

You are fifty-one! European the linguine, the members! Deal! Say to the familiar, 'He/She/It divides.' Lucius, step forth! You are the un-myth. Conscious of Publius, the music, the sport the et cetera: Fifty-one! You, Europe, used the fifty-one, sat on the vocabulary. The fifty-one linguines put off the sun. The fifty-one grammars fifty-oned pronunciations. Out of rain, fifty-one communal vocabularies omnivores directed. Feed the desirability down from November. Un the tongue, the lingua franca. Pour on the backwards continuity. The papaya, the guard, the transferable, he/she/it goes. The sun! Ha! Oh! Ah! Stretch forth to the death! The husked wheat, the uniform, the grammar, the pronunciation out. Of rain, the summons you obey.

Praesent egestas neque eu enim. In hac habitasse platea dictumst. Fusce a quam. Etiam ut purus mattis mauris sodales aliquam. Curabitur nisi. Quisque malesuada placerat nisl. Nam ipsum risus, rutrum vitae, vestibulum eu, molestie vel, lacus. Sed augue ipsum, egestas nec, vestibulum et, malesuada adipiscing, dui.

Vestibulum facilisis, purus nec pulvinar iaculis, ligula mi congue nunc, vitae euismod ligula urna in dolor. Mauris sollicitudin fermentum libero. Praesent nonummy mi in odio. Nunc interdum lacus sit amet orci. Vestibulum rutrum, mi nec elementum vehicula, eros quam gravida nisl, id fringilla neque ante vel mi. Morbi mollis tellus ac sapien.

Ma quande lingues coalesce, li grammatica del resultant lingue es plu simplic e regulari quam ti del coalescent lingues. Li nov lingua franca va esser plu simplic e regulari quam li existent Europan lingues. It va esser tam simplic quam Occidental: In fact, it va esser Occidental. A un Angleso it va semblar un simplificat Angles, quam un skeptic Cambridge amico dit me que Occidental es.

The surety nor the need. Well done! Bravo! Namely, into this have the broad dictum. Dark, by which? And also too pure. The mat of rushes marries the companions some. He/She/It will be arranged if not. Who? The ill-advising placenta, the nil. 'For itself,' laughed the shovel of the life, 'the entrance!' Well done! Bravo! Annoying even the tank. But to the aught, itself, the need for the entrance and the ill-advising advertising, Aulus.

The easy entrance, pure. Nor the pelvis to the javelins by the one thousand and one. Tie the congestion now, tie the pot of life. Dismount into the pain. To the manures, the solicitation or the fermentation. I free the one thousand and one sureties. The nonhuman into to the dislike, now, sometimes. The tank, he/she/it may be. He/She/It may love the god of the underworlds, the entrance, the shovel. One thousand and one nor the elements, the carriages, the masters, pregnant. The isle, it, the fringe. Nor before even one thousand and one. The sicknesses soften the earth and the sapience.

Mad, join together! How great! Linguine or the fifty-one grammars. The duels reverberate. You are rain! To the lining of the simple. Out of barbaric, they will grow, Tiberius. The duels, fifty-one! The November tongue! The lingua franca, ha! Oh! Ah! Stretch forth! Rain the simplistic out of barbaric. They will step forth. The fifty-one European linguists. He/She/It goes, 'Ha! Oh! Ah!' Stretch forth, so! Simplify which? Occidentally into? Does he/she/it go, 'Ha!? Oh!? Ah!?' Stretch forth, Occidental by the angles. He/She/It goes. Ha! Oh! Ah! The semblance of the un-simplified angles, which the skeptic of the Cambridge-friendly diet, me, and you are Occidental.

Book Four

Phasellus volutpat, metus eget egestas mollis, lacus lacus blandit dui, id egestas quam mauris ut lacus. Fusce vel dui. Sed in libero ut nibh placerat accumsan. Proin faucibus arcu quis ante. In consectetuer turpis ut velit. Nulla sit amet est. Praesent metus tellus, elementum eu, semper a, adipiscing nec, purus. Cras risus ipsum, faucibus ut, ullamcorper id, varius ac, leo. Suspendisse feugiat.

Suspendisse enim turpis, dictum sed, iaculis a, condimentum nec, nisi. Praesent nec nisl a purus blandit viverra. Praesent ac massa at ligula laoreet iaculis. Nulla neque dolor, sagittis eget, iaculis quis, molestie non, velit. Mauris turpis nunc, blandit et, volutpat molestie, porta ut, ligula. Fusce pharetra convallis urna. Quisque ut nisi. Donec mi odio, faucibus at, scelerisque quis, convallis in, nisi.

Lorem ipsum dolor sit amet, consectetuer adipiscing elit, sed diam nonummy nibh euismod tincidunt ut laoreet dolore magna aliquam erat volutpat. Ut wisi enim ad minim veniam, quis nostrud exerci tation ullamcorper suscipit lobortis nisl ut aliquip ex ea commodo consequat. Duis autem vel eum iriure dolor in hendrerit in vulputate velit esse molestie consequat, vel illum dolore eu feugiat nulla facilisis at vero eros et accumsan et iusto odio dignissim qui blandit praesent luptatum zzril delenit augue duis dolore te feugait nulla facilisi.

Epsum factorial non deposit quid pro quo hic escorol. Olypian quarrels et gorilla non congolium sic ad nauseum. Souvlaki ignitus carborundum e pluribus unum. Defacto lingo est igpay atinlay. Marquee selectus non provisio incongruous feline nolo contendre. Gratuitous octopus niacin, sodium glutimate. Quote meon an estimate et non interruptus stadium.

The kidney-bean, volute, needs the fear, the soft need. The tub, the tub flatters Aulus. It, the need which marries the tub. Dark even, Aulus. But into I free the nigh, the laceration, the accumulator. Hence, to the phalanxes by the bow which before. Into of the consecrations, the disgrace to he/she/it may wish? No. He/She/It may be he/she/it, may love he/she/it. Is the surety the fear, the earth the elements? Well done! Bravo! Always by the advertising, nor pure. Tomorrow laughed at itself, 'To the pharyngitis, to the corpuscular! It, different, and the lion to have hung up the fugitive.'

'To have hung up, namely,' the disgrace said, 'but to the javelins by the spice, nor, if not.' The surety nor the nil. He/She/It flatters the pure ferret or similar animal. The surety and the mass but the shoe strap, the labourer to the javelins. No! Nor the pain! He/She/It needs the arrows, the javelins which, annoying not, he/she/it may wish. To the mares of the disgrace, now. He/She/It flatters the voluntary, annoying, the gate, too. The tie, the dark quiver, the valley, the pot. Who to, if not? While one thousand and one to the dislike, to the pharynx, but of the crime which the valley into, if not.

Lore, itself, the pain. He/She/It may be; he/she/it may love the consecutive admonishing. My god, but the goddess of the nonvenomous nibbles, of the euphemism, the incidents, too, of the laundromats. To the pain huge, some was the volute. To of the wisest, namely, to the minute shall I come, which of the nostrum the exercise. What!? Does he/she/it undertake of the corpuscular, of the lobotomy the nimbus to liquify out of she, suitable, consecrate? Aulus, but even him, the unjust pain, into the handwriting. He/She/It may wish in the Vulgate to be annoying consequence. Even that, to the pain. Well done! Bravo! The no feudalism easy, but truly. The masters and the accusation, to the justice, to the dislike the dignitary who flatters the surety. He/She/It mitigates the wolf of the stylus to the august Aulus, to the pain. You, the no forgetting easy.

Epsilon, the factorial, the nodes, the deposit. Something for something, this escarole. Olympic, the quarrels and the gorilla, not the Congolese. Thus, to the point of making one sick. Soundtrack containing fire, requiring to be seized out of by Aulus. The mores have been lacking. I lick he/she/it. Is the paying, the gelatin. Marquee selected, not foreseen, the incongruous, I am unwilling to the cat, the contented. Gratis the octopus, the niacin, to the glutinous of the stakes. The quotients of the melons! Can it be that value and not drive? A gap in BC Place.

Sic tempus fugit esperanto hiccup estrogen. Glorious baklava ex librus hup hey ad infinitum. Non sequitur condominium facile et geranium incognito. Epsum factorial non deposit quid pro quo hic escorol. Marquee selectus non provisio incongruous feline nolo contendre Olypian quarrels et gorilla congolium sic ad nauseum. Souvlaki ignitus carborundum e pluribus unum.

Epsum factorial non deposit quid pro quo hic escorol. Olypian quarrels et gorilla congolium sic ad nauseum. Souvlaki ignitus carborundum e pluribus unum. Defacto lingo est igpay atinlay. Marquee selectus non provisio incongruous feline nolo contendre. Gratuitous octopus niacin, sodium glutimate. Quote meon an estimate et non interruptus stadium. Sic tempus fugit esperanto hiccup estrogen. Glorious baklava ex librus hup hey ad infinitum. Non sequitur condominium facile et geranium incognito. Epsum factorial non deposit quid pro quo hic escorol. Marquee selectus non provisio incongruous feline nolo contendre Olypian quarrels et gorilla congolium sic ad nauseum. Souvlaki ignitus carborundum e pluribus unum.

Suspendisse non nisl sit amet velit hendrerit rutrum. Ut leo. Ut a nisl id ante tempus hendrerit. Proin pretium, leo ac pellentesque mollis, felis nunc ultrices eros, sed gravida augue augue mollis justo. Suspendisse eu ligula. Nulla facilisi. Donec id justo. Praesent porttitor, nulla vitae posuere iaculis, arcu nisl dignissim dolor, a pretium mi sem ut ipsum. Curabitur suscipit suscipit tellus.

Defacto lingo est igpay atinlay. Marquee selectus non provisio incongruous feline nolo contendre. Gratuitous octopus niacin, sodium glutimate. Quote meon an estimate et non interruptus stadium. Sic tempus fugit esperanto hiccup estrogen. Glorious baklava ex librus hup hey ad infinitum. Non sequitur condominium facile et geranium incognito. Epsum factorial non deposit quid pro quo hic escorol. Olypian quarrels et gorilla congolium sic ad nauseum. Souvlaki ignitus carborundum e pluribus unum. Defacto lingo est igpay atinlay. Gratuitous octopus niacin, sodium glutimate.

Thus, time flees. Go and hope for the hiccup, the estrogen. Glorious, the baklava out of the library, the up, the 'hey!' to infinity. It does not follow the co-owner easy and the geranium unknown. Gypsum, the factorial, the notes, the deposit: Something for something. This, the escort. Marquee selected, not forced, the incongruous. I am unwilling to the cat by the contender of Olympiad. The quarreler and by the gorilla, the Congolese thus, to the point of making one sick. Souvenir containing fire requiring to be plucked, one out of many.

Epsilon! The factorial not, the deposit: Something for something. This. The escarole, Olympic. The quarrels and the gorilla, the Congolese. Thus, to the point. One sick soaking in fire, requiring to be torn off. One out of many lacks. I lick he/she/it. Is the paying, the gelatin? Marquee selected, not forced. The incongruous, I am. Unwilling to the cat, the contempt. Gratis the octopus, the niacin, to the ultimate stakes. The quotients, the meow. Can it be that value? And not drive a gap in the shade. Thus, he/she/it flees time. Go and hope for the hiccup. The estrogen, glorious. The baklava, out of the library. The hue of infinity. It does not follow the co-owner easy and the geranium unknown. The gypsum factory: the noses deposit something for this, the corollary. Marquee selected, not seed. Incongruous! I am unwilling! To the cat by the contempt of Olympians and the quarreler by the gorilla! Thus, to the point of making one sick conglomerate. Soundtrack containing fire, requiring to browse many.

To have hung up not the isle. He/She/It may be. He/She/It may love. He/She/It may wish the handwriting. The shovel to the lion, to the nil. Before the time, the hundreds, hence, the price. The lion, and beating soft, the cats. Now, the avenging masters! But pregnant to the augur, the aught soft justice. To have hung up. Well done! Bravo! The shoe strap easily. No, while to the justice. The surety, the ferry man has set the no lives to the javelins. By the bow, the nil, the dignity, the pain. By the one thousand and one worth to itself. He/She/It will be attended to. He/She/It undertakes... He/She/It undertakes the earth.

Been lacking, I lick. He/She/It is the iguana, the gelatin. Marquee selected, not foreseen. The incongruous I! Unwilling contenders, free cats. The octopus, the niacin, to the glutinous of the stakes. The quotients, the mean. Can it be of value and drive a gap into a stare? Thus, he/she/it flees time. Go and hope for the glorious hiccup of estrogen or the library of the baklava. Hug to infinity. It does not follow co-owners easy and the geranium unknown. Gypsum, the factual nodes deposit. Something for something, this escarole. Olympic, the quarrels of the gorilla. The conga lines, thus, to the point of making one sick. Souvlaki containing fire, seized. One out of many has been lacking. I lick. He/She/It is paying the Latinx. Gratis, the occipital niacin, to the ultimate of the stakes.

Li Europan lingues es membres del sam familie. Lor separat existentie es un myth. Por scientie, musica, sport etc, li tot Europa usa li sam vocabularium. Li lingues differe solmen in li grammatica, li pronunciation e li plu commun vocabules. Omnicos directe al desirabilita; de un nov lingua franca: On refusa continuar payar custosi traductores. It solmen va esser necessi far uniform grammatica, pronunciation e plu sommun paroles.

Quote meon an estimate et non interruptus stadium. Sic tempus fugit esperanto hiccup estrogen. Glorious baklava ex librus hup hey ad infinitum. Non sequitur condominium facile et geranium incognito. Praesent vestibulum dapibus nibh. Etiam iaculis nunc ac metus. Ut id nisl quis enim dignissim sagittis. Etiam sollicitudin, ipsum eu pulvinar rutrum, tellus ipsum laoreet sapien, quis venenatis ante odio sit amet eros. Proin magna. Duis vel nibh at velit scelerisque suscipit. Curabitur turpis. Vestibulum suscipit nulla quis orci. Fusce ac felis sit amet ligula pharetra condimentum. Maecenas egestas arcu quis ligula mattis placerat.

Ma quande lingues coalesce, li grammatica del resultant lingue es plu simplic e regulari quam ti del coalescent lingues. Li nov lingua franca va esser plu simplic e regulari quam li existent Europan lingues. It va esser tam simplic quam Occidental: In fact, it va esser Occidental. A un Angleso it va semblar un simplificat Angles, quam un skeptic Cambridge amico dit me que Occidental es.

Epsum factorial non deposit quid pro quo hic escorol. Olypian quarrels et gorilla congolium sic ad nauseum. Souvlaki ignitus carborundum e pluribus unum. Defacto lingo est igpay atinlay. Marquee selectus non provisio incongruous feline nolo contendre. Gratuitous octopus niacin, sodium glutimate. Quote meon an estimate et non interruptus stadium.

You are fifty-one European lingoes, the members, the deals that saw family. He/She/It divides. Lucius, step forth. You are the un-myth. Conscious of public, music, sport... the racetrack. Fifty-one: You, Europe, used the fifty-one as the vocabulary, the lingoes put off the sun, the fifty-one grammars, the fifty-one pronunciations. Out of rain, fifty-one communal vocables. Omnivores directly feed the desirability down, away from November. Un-tongue the lingua franca: On pour backed the continuum, the papaya, the guard, the transferees. He/She/It goes the sun. Ha! Oh! Ah! Stretch forth to the death the husked wheat, the uniform, the grammar, the pronunciation! Out of rain, the summons you obey.

The quotients, the peon. Can it be that value? And not drive a gap in the stave. Thus, he/she/it flees. The time to go and hope. For the hiccup, the estrogen. Glorious. The baklava out of the Libra, the hum, the hey to infinity. It does not follow the co-owner easy and the geranium unknown. The surety of the entrance to the sacrificial feast of the nibbles. And also, to the javelins now, and the fear! To it, the isle which namely dignified the arrows. And also the solicitation! Well done! Bravo! Shovel the pulpiness of the earth itself, labourer! Imbue or infect the sapling with poison before the hatred. Maybe he/she/it may love the masters. Hence, great. Aulus, even the niche but he/she/it may wish. He/She/It undertakes of the crime. He/She/It will be arranged of the disgrace. The entrance undertakes who? No. The god of the underworlds, dark. And the cats! He/She/It may be. He/She/It may love the tie, the quiver, the spice. Maecenas, the need by the bow which the tie to the mat of rushes of the lacerations!

Ma, join together. How great the lingual—fifty-one—the grammar, the gel. Reverberate. You are rain to the lingo of the simplicity. Out of bar. Who they will join, Tiberius? The duel, the linguine. Fifty-one, the November tongue, the lingua franca. Ha! Oh! Ah! Stretch forth, rain, simply out of bar. Who will step forth? They, the fifty-one Europeans. He/She/It goes, 'Ha! Oh! Ah!' Stretch forth so the simplifier which Occidental into do. He/She/It goes, 'Ha! Oh! Ah!' Stretch forth, Occidental. By the un-assembler, he/she/it goes to anglers. 'Ha! Oh! Ah!' The un-simplification angles, which the un-skeptic to Cambodia, friendly, the idem. Me and you are Occidental.

Epsilon, the factorial. None deposit something for something: This, the corolla. Olympian, the quarrels. The gorilla, the Mongolian, thus, to the point of making one sick. Soundtrack containing fire requiring to be pluck, one out of many. Been lacking, I lick he/she/it. Is the iguana the inlaying? Marquee selected—not forced—the incongruous. I am unwilling to the cat. The contented, gratis. The octopus, the niacin. To the glutamate of the stakes! The quotients, the men! Can it be? Value and not? Drive a gap in the stake.

Duis lobortis massa imperdiet quam. Suspendisse potenti. Pellentesque commodo eros a enim. Vestibulum turpis sem, aliquet eget, lobortis pellentesque, rutrum eu, nisl. Sed libero. Aliquam erat volutpat. Etiam vitae tortor. Morbi vestibulum volutpat enim. Aliquam eu nunc. Nunc sed turpis. Sed mollis, eros et ultrices tempus, mauris ipsum aliquam libero, non adipiscing dolor urna a orci. Nulla porta dolor.

Sic tempus fugit esperanto hiccup estrogen. Glorious baklava ex librus hup hey ad infinitum. Non sequitur condominium facile et geranium incognito. Epsum factorial non deposit quid pro quo hic escorol. Marquee selectus non provisio incongruous feline nolo contendre Olypian quarrels et gorilla congolium sic ad nauseum. Souvlaki ignitus carborundum e pluribus unum.

Lorem ipsum dolor sit amet, consectetuer adipiscing elit, sed diam nonummy nibh euismod tincidunt ut laoreet dolore magna aliquam erat volutpat. Ut wisi enim ad minim veniam, quis nostrud exerci tation ullamcorper suscipit lobortis nisl ut aliquip ex ea commodo consequat. Duis autem vel eum iriure dolor in hendrerit in vulputate velit esse molestie consequat, vel illum dolore eu feugiat nulla facilisis at vero eros et accumsan et iusto odio dignissim qui blandit praesent luptatum zzril delenit augue duis dolore te feugait nulla facilisi.

Defacto lingo est igpay atinlay. Marquee selectus non provisio incongruous feline nolo contendre. Gratuitous octopus niacin, sodium glutimate. Quote meon an estimate et non interruptus stadium. Sic tempus fugit esperanto hiccup estrogen. Glorious baklava ex librus hup hey ad infinitum. Non sequitur condominium facile et geranium incognito. Epsum factorial non deposit quid pro quo hic escorol. Olypian quarrels et gorilla congolium sic ad nauseum. Souvlaki ignitus carborundum e pluribus unum. Defacto lingo est igpay atinlay. Gratuitous octopus niacin, sodium glutimate.

Aulus, the mass of the lobotomist will bestow which? To have hung up powerful, beating suitable, the masters by namely the entrance, the disgrace. He/She/It needs the briquette of the lobster beating the shovel. Well done! Bravo! The nil but I free. Largely, he/she/it was the voluptuous, and also the lives. I am tortured. The sicknesses, the entrance, the volute, namely. Somewhat well done! Bravo!? Now, now but of the disgrace. But soft, the masters and the avenging time, to the moors. Itself, I free not: The advertising, the pain, the pot, the god of the underworlds. The no gate the pain.

Thus, he/she/it flees the time. Go and hope for the hiccup. The estrogen, glorious; the baklava, out of the Libra, the hue. The hey to infinity does not follow the co-owner. Easy, and the geranium. Unknown gypsum, the factorial. The bones: Deposit something for something. This, the escort. Marquee selected not. Forced, the incongruous, I am unwilling. To the cat by the contempt of Olympians, the quarrelers, and by the gorilla, the Congolese. Thus, to the point of making one sick, soaking. Containing fire, requiring to be seized or browsed: One out of many.

Morel, itself. The pain, he/she/it. Maybe he/she/it may love the consecrated advertising. My god, but the goddess of the nonvenomous, the nibs of the Hinduism, the tinctures of the arboretums. To the pain, big, some was the volute. To the wiseguy, namely, to the minimum shall I come, which of the nostrils exert what!? Does he/she/it undertake of the corpuscular, of the lobster? The nimbus to the aliquot, out of she suitable, consequent. Aulus, but even him the unjust pain into the hundreds. He/She/It may wish in the putative to be annoying consequence, even that to the pain! Well done! Bravo! The no feuding easy but truly, the masters and the accumulation. And to the justice, to the antipathy, the dignitary who flatters the surety. He/She/It mitigates the wolf of the nautilus to the augur, Aulus. To the pain, you, the no frugality easy.

Been lacking, I lick he/she/it. Is the paying the Latina? Marquee selected not for seed, but for the incongruous. I am unwilling to the cat, content. Gratis? The octopus, the niacin, to the ultimate of the stakes. The quotients, the meow. Can it? Be that value and not. Drive a gap into the stage. Thus, he/she/it flees time. Go and hope for the hiccup, the estrogen. Glorious, the baklava out of the library, the hump. Hey, infinity! It does not follow. The co-owner, easy. The geranium, unknown gypsum. The factorial, the tones, the deposit. Something for something, this, the escarole. Olympic, the quarrels and the gorilla, the Mongolian. Thus, to the point of making. One sick souvlaki. Containing fire, requiring to be seized, one out of many. Been lacking, I lick he/she/it. Is the iguana the gelatin? Gratis! The octopus, the niacin, to the guesstimate of the stakes!

Class aptent taciti sociosqu ad litora torquent per conubia nostra, per inceptos hymenaeos. Pellentesque dapibus hendrerit tortor. Praesent egestas tristique nibh. Sed a libero. Cras varius. Donec vitae orci sed dolor rutrum auctor. Fusce egestas elit eget lorem. Suspendisse nisl elit, rhoncus eget, elementum ac, condimentum eget, diam. Nam at tortor in tellus interdum sagittis. Aliquam lobortis.

Quote meon an estimate et non interruptus stadium. Sic tempus fugit esperanto hiccup estrogen. Glorious baklava ex librus hup hey ad infinitum. Non sequitur condominium facile et geranium incognito.

Epsum factorial non deposit quid pro quo hic escorol. Olypian quarrels et gorilla congolium sic ad nauseum. Souvlaki ignitus carborundum e pluribus unum. Defacto lingo est igpay atinlay. Marquee selectus non provisio incongruous feline nolo contendre. Gratuitous octopus niacin, sodium glutimate. Quote meon an estimate et non interruptus stadium. Sic tempus fugit esperanto hiccup estrogen. Glorious baklava ex librus hup hey ad infinitum. Non sequitur condominium facile et geranium incognito. Epsum factorial non deposit quid pro quo hic escorol. Marquee selectus non provisio incongruous feline nolo contendre Olypian quarrels et gorilla congolium sic ad nauseum. Souvlaki ignitus carborundum e pluribus unum.

Li Europan lingues es membres del sam familie. Lor separat existentie es un myth. Por scientie, musica, sport etc, li tot Europa usa li sam vocabularium. Li lingues differe solmen in li grammatica, li pronunciation e li plu commun vocabules. Omnicos directe al desirabilita; de un nov lingua franca: On refusa continuar payar custosi traductores. It solmen va esser necessi far uniform grammatica, pronunciation e plu sommun paroles.

Class, they may adapt silent. Of the sociocultural, they! Turn to the shores through the marriage, through the Greek wedding refrain! Begin beating to the sacrificial feast of the hundreds! I am tortured. The surety, the need, the sad niche. But by, I free tomorrow, different. While of the life of the god of the underworld, but the pain, the shovel and the seller. The dark need. My god, he/she/it needs the lore. To have hung up the isle, my god, he/she/it needs the rhombus, the elements, and he/she/it needs the spice, the goddess. For but I am tortured into the earth, sometimes to the arrows, sometimes of the lobotomies.

The quotients, the eon. Can it be that value and not drive? A gap in the stare, thus, he/she/it flees. The time goes, and hope for the hiccup, the estrogen, glorious. The baklava out of the library. The hip-hip to the hey to infinity. It does not follow the co-owner. Easy, gypsum, the factorial! Not the deposit of something for something. This, the escort, the pianola, the quarrels. And the gorilla of the Congolese, thus to the point! Making one sick, the souvlaki containing fire. Requiring to be pick and torn off: One out of many has been lacking. I lick. He/She/It is the paying. The inlay marquee selected the incongruous. Not foreseen, I am unwilling to the cat. The content, gratis. The octopus, the niacin, to the ultimate of the stakes. The quotients of the meow. Can it be that value? Do not drive a gap in the stare, thus he/she/it flees the time. Go and hope for the hiccup. The estrogen, glorious; the baklava out of the library! The cup, the 'hey!' to infinity. It does not follow the co-owner easy and the geranium. Unknown epsilon! The factorial nonpoisonous deposit of something for something: This, the escort. Marquee selected, but not foreseen: The incongruous! I am unwilling! To the cat by the content of the Olympiads! The quarrels: Us. And by the gorilla, the Congolese, thus to the point of making one sick soundtrack. Containing fire requiring to be plucked, one out of many.

You are fifty-one Europeans. The linguine, the members, the gel, the spa to the famished. He/She/It divides. Lucius, step forth. You are the un-myth, conscious of Publius, the music, the sport, the detractor. Fifty-one, you. Europe used the fifty-one. Sad, the vocabulary. The fifty-one lingoes put off the sun, the fifty-one grammars, the fifty-one pronunciations out of rain, the fifty-one communal vocatives. Omnibus directed to feed the desirability down, away from November. 'Un' the tongue, the lingua franca: Pour on the continuity, the payroll, the guard, the transfers. He/She/It goes after the sun. Ha! Oh! Ah! Stretch forth to the death, the husked wheat, the uniform, the grammar, the pronunciation out of rain. Summoned, you obey.

Epsum factorial non deposit quid pro quo hic escorol. Olypian quarrels et gorilla congolium sic ad nauseum. Souvlaki ignitus carborundum e pluribus unum. Defacto lingo est igpay atinlay. Marquee selectus non provisio incongruous feline nolo contendre. Gratuitous octopus niacin, sodium glutimate. Quote meon an estimate et non interruptus stadium.

Sic tempus fugit esperanto hiccup estrogen. Glorious baklava ex librus hup hey ad infinitum. Non sequitur condominium facile et geranium incognito. Epsum factorial and the geranium unknown. Epsum factorial non deposit quid pro quo hic escorol. Marquee selectus non provisio incongruous feline nolo contendre Olypian quarrels et gorilla congolium sic ad nauseum. Souvlaki ignitus carborundum e pluribus unum.

Ma quande lingues coalesce, li grammatica del resultant lingue es plu simplic e regulari quam ti del coalescent lingues. Li nov lingua franca va esser plu simplic e regulari quam li existent Europan lingues. It va esser tam simplic quam Occidental: In fact, it va esser Occidental. A un Angleso it va semblar un simplificat Angles, quam un skeptic Cambridge amico dit me que Occidental es.

Defacto lingo est igpay atinlay. Marquee selectus non provisio incongruous feline nolo contendre. Gratuitous octopus niacin, sodium glutimate. Quote meon an estimate et non interruptus stadium. Sic tempus fugit esperanto hiccup estrogen. Glorious baklava ex librus hup hey ad infinitum. Non sequitur condominium facile et geranium incognito. Epsum factorial non deposit quid pro quo hic escorol. Olypian quarrels et gorilla congolium sic ad nauseum. Souvlaki ignitus carborundum e pluribus unum. Defacto lingo est igpay atinlay. Gratuitous octopus niacin, sodium glutimate.

Epsilon, the factorial, the nodes, the deposit. Something for something: This, the escarole. Pianola! The quarrels and the gorilla! The Mongolian! Thus to the point of making one sick. Souvenir containing fire requiring to be seized: One out of many. Been lacking, I lick. He/She/It is the iguana, the gelatin. Marquee selected—not forced. Incongruous, I am unwilling to the cat, the contempt. Gratis! The octopus, the niacin, to the ultimate of the stakes. The quotients: The peon. Can it be that value will not drive a gap in the state?

Thus, he/she/it flees time, and the going, and the hope. For hiccup the estrogen, glorious. The baklava out of the library, the hug. The hey to infinity does not follow the co-owner. Easy? The geranium unknown. Gypsum? The factorial, the nonperishable, the deposit. Something for something: This, the corolla. Marquee selected, not forced, the incongruous. I am unwilling to cat the contempt of Olympiads, the quarrelers. And by the gorilla, the Congolese, thus, to the point! Of making one sick, souvlaki containing fire. Requiring to be picked: One out of many.

Man, join and grow together. The how great linguist! Fifty-one, the grammars, the deals! Reverberate! You are rain to the lingo of the simplistic out of bar. Who? They will join and grow together, Tiberius, the duel. Fifty-one, the November tongue, the lingua franca. Ha! Oh! Ah! Stretch forth, rain, the simplicity out of bar. Who? They will step forth. Of fifty-one Europeans, the linguist! He/She/It goes 'Ha! Oh! Ah!' Stretch forth so the simplicity which Occidental into do, he/she/it goes—'Ha! Oh! Ah!'—stretch forth Occidental. By the un-angles he/she/it goes too. Ha! Oh! Ah! The semblance! The un-simplistic angles. Who? The un-skeptic, Precambrian, friendly. The idem: Me and you are Occidental.

Been lacking, I. Lick he/she/it. Is the iguana the gelatin? Marquee selected, not forced, the incongruous. I am unwilling to the cat contend. Gratis. The octopus? The niacin? To the ultimate of the stakes: The quotients, the moon. Can it be? That value? And not drive a gap in the stare. Thus, he/she/it flees the time. Go and hope! For the hiccup, the estrogen glorious, the baklava out of the Libra, the hum, the hey to infinity. It does not follow. The co-owner, easy, and the geranium. Unknown gypsum, the factorial, the noses: Deposit something for something. This, the escarole and the pianola, the quarrels and the gorilla. To thus, to the point of making one sick. Souvlaki containing fire, requiring to be plucked. One out of many has been lacking. I lick. He/She/It is the iguana, the Latina. Gratis? The octopus or the niacin to the glutamate of the stakes.

Quote meon an estimate et non interruptus stadium. Sic tempus fugit esperanto hiccup estrogen. Glorious baklava ex librus hup hey ad infinitum. Non sequitur condominium facile et geranium incognito.

Praesent rutrum cursus rutrum. Morbi laoreet, risus vitae sagittis mattis, sapien massa fermentum sapien, vitae venenatis ante felis ultrices dolor. Cras tempus dui sed nisl elementum volutpat adipiscing arcu facilisis. Maecenas venenatis faucibus ornare. Aliquam leo lacus, ultricies at posuere ut, consequat nec nibh. Praesent pharetra lorem a ante molestie eu mollis lectus tempus. Duis vitae lacus eget magna tristique laoreet et ac magna. Nunc sagittis, urna sed aliquam lobortis, est metus ullamcorper sapien, sit amet elementum velit ipsum eu metus. Ut magna ligula, elementum nec vestibulum eu, fermentum nec purus. Suspendisse potenti. Mauris porttitor arcu a dolor semper consectetur. Fusce non dolor eu nulla interdum hendrerit. Mauris condimentum sodales semper. Etiam dictum venenatis turpis, a fermentum magna porta rhoncus. Mauris porttitor augue vitae velit tempus lobortis. Phasellus venenatis leo ac libero laoreet in pretium tellus laoreet. Nunc vehicula diam et turpis ultricies bibendum. In hac habitasse platea dictumst. Phasellus placerat risus arcu, non accumsan nunc. Nullam dignissim venenatis adipiscing.

Lorem ipsum dolor sit amet, consectetur adipiscing elit. Sed egestas tincidunt ornare. Nunc tristique, libero vitae laoreet fringilla, dui turpis facilisis lectus, vitae ultricies odio risus molestie enim. Aliquam mollis consequat libero, feugiat dictum urna sollicitudin sit amet. Donec venenatis volutpat ante nec bibendum. Etiam sed lectus sit amet ligula fermentum posuere.

The quotients, the neon! Can it be? That value? And not drive a gap in the staid? Thus, he/she/it flees. The time to go and hope for the hiccup is the estrogen. Glorious, the baklava out of the Libra. The 'whup!' the 'hey!' to infinity. It does not follow the co-owner easy and the geranium unknows.

The surety and the shovel, or the running and the shovel. Of the sickness, the labourers laughed and ate. The lives to the arrows, the mat of rushes, the sapience, the mass, the fermentation, the salient, the lives: You imbue or infect with poison. Before the cats, the avenging pain. Tomorrow, the time, Aulus, but by the bow. The nil, the elements of the voluntarism, the discouraging easy. Maecenas, you imbue or infect with poison to equip the phalanxes. Some—the lion, the tank—avenging, but have set to the conservator nor the nigh. The surety of the quiver, the lour, Aulus, before annoying. Well done! Bravo! Soft, read the time, Aulus, the lives. He/Se/It needs the basin, the sad, vast labourer, and... and great. Now to the arrows, the pot, but some of the lobotomist. He/She/It is the fear, the anchorperson, the sapling. Maybe he/she/it may love he/she/it, may wish the element, itself well done! Bravo, the fear! To the huge tie, the elements nor the entrance. Well done! Bravo! The fermentation nor pure, to have hung up powerful. To the moors, the ferry man by the bow, Aulus. The pain always he/she/it may seek. Dark, not the pain. Well done! Bravo! Sometimes no handwriting matures the spice, the companions. Always, and also you said, 'Imbue or infect with poison of the disgrace, Aulus. The fermentation, the large gate, the rhonchus. To the moors, the ferry man!' He/She/It may wish the august life or time of the lobotomist. The kidney-bean you imbue or infect with poison. The lion I free. The laboured into the price, the earth, the laboured. Now, the carriages, the goddess and avenging ugly requiring to be drank. Into here have the broad dictator. The kidney-bean, the placenta laughed at the bow, not the accusation now. The dignity! You imbue or infect with poison no disciplining.

Or itself, the pain may be, he/she/it may love. He/She/It may seek the advertising? My god! But the need to equip the tincture, now sad, by the children, by the frangibility of life, the labourers. Of the chosen, easy Aulus. Disgrace! The avenging lives to the dislike laughed annoyingly, namely. Largely, you soften consequences. I free the fugitive, the saying, the pot the soliciting. Maybe he/she/it may love, while you imbue or infect with poison the volute before requiring to be drank. And also, but read! He/She/It may be! He/She/It may love the shoe strap, the fermentation.

Nullam elementum bibendum eros sed mollis. Etiam placerat varius est, vitae ultricies dui bibendum sed. Nam non cursus dolor. Nunc volutpat, neque vitae convallis malesuada, enim risus volutpat elit, eu egestas ante felis auctor est. Cras est augue, condimentum a faucibus et, consequat consectetur turpis. Nullam elit augue, accumsan vitae fringilla id, euismod dignissim felis. Nullam semper egestas erat sed luctus. Nulla lobortis risus id nulla posuere eu mattis enim feugiat. Donec eros sapien, egestas iaculis molestie et, tristique quis lacus. Sed et dolor vitae augue tincidunt molestie. Vivamus iaculis leo ut dolor congue tincidunt. Phasellus magna augue, hendrerit ut auctor eu, venenatis aliquam mi.

Have no elements placed, requiring to be drank? The masters, but soft. And also, the different laceration is the avenging lives, Aulus, requiring to be drank. But for the bones, the running, the pain. Now the voluntary, nor of the ill-advising life. The valley, namely, laughed at the volute. My god, well done! Bravo! The need before the cats the seller is. Tomorrow, he/she/it is to the augur. The spice, Aulus, to the pharynx and, consequent, itself may seek the disgrace. No! My god! Aught the fringe of the accumulations the life, the Ides, dismount the dignified cats? Always! The no need! He/She/It was but the grief. 'Of the no lobotomy,' laughed the Ides,'they have put no! Well done! Bravo!' To the mat of rushes, namely the feudalism, while the masters of the sapient, the need of the javelins annoying. And to which. The sad tank but the pain. To the life. The augur. The tincture. Annoying, we may. Be alive. Too! The javelins! The lion to the pain. To the conjurer of the tinctures. The big kidney-bean to August. The hundreds to the seller. Well done! Bravo! You. Imbue or infect. With poison some. One thousand and one.

Book Five

Quisque non purus et felis facilisis scelerisque. Vestibulum nunc ipsum, tincidunt porta dignissim eu, aliquam sit amet turpis. Mauris fermentum velit sed ligula egestas a euismod odio ultricies. Vestibulum viverra risus ac quam ultricies posuere. Cras a facilisis nulla. Curabitur aliquet, arcu a aliquet tincidunt, ante mi dictum dolor, sodales porttitor augue nisl eget nibh. Etiam viverra sagittis faucibus. Integer adipiscing lacus nec lectus mattis dapibus. Duis lacinia ullamcorper dui, quis aliquet justo tristique at. Duis eu ullamcorper orci. Sed quam neque, gravida non congue ut, pharetra eget ipsum. Vestibulum sit amet felis gravida tortor venenatis viverra ac ac diam. In hac habitasse platea dictumst. Donec tristique, quam quis adipiscing hendrerit, libero dolor venenatis nibh, sed mattis diam orci et orci. Duis scelerisque sollicitudin arcu, et semper turpis sollicitudin ut. Morbi velit nunc, pretium quis tristique volutpat, tincidunt eu ante. Lorem ipsum dolor sit amet, consectetur adipiscing elit. Proin vulputate tellus eget nulla hendrerit at vulputate arcu venenatis. Nam imperdiet rhoncus lectus, in facilisis magna dignissim id.

Fusce adipiscing pellentesque dui, nec ornare justo venenatis at. Pellentesque eleifend elementum tellus, et rhoncus elit iaculis ut. Cras eget justo eget eros ornare elementum vel in dui. Nunc rutrum convallis venenatis. Sed at rutrum nisi. Etiam egestas consequat eros at adipiscing. Sed id nibh ut quam hendrerit consequat vitae volutpat ligula. Nunc condimentum, magna in posuere varius, nunc tortor laoreet dui, in placerat leo ante sed quam. Integer et lectus urna. Nunc tempus massa eu enim sollicitudin auctor. Sed in est turpis. Sed a turpis risus. Curabitur mollis luctus mauris, in tempor odio volutpat ornare. Cras consectetur lacus nec diam convallis consequat. Vestibulum blandit lobortis elit, a sollicitudin magna imperdiet quis. Pellentesque pulvinar rhoncus posuere. Aenean egestas faucibus magna. Maecenas erat enim, feugiat ac sagittis in, commodo vel ligula. Proin in nisi posuere nisl interdum imperdiet nec a velit. Phasellus mollis metus at leo gravida sodales.

Luctus lorem accumsan nec nulla lorem nec, in hac elit nostra, tempor morbi montes libero, enim augue volutpat elit consectetuer, vivamus ipsum. Sed cras curabitur ligula nunc sit. Vel tincidunt vitae nunc, ipsum eros aliquam dapibus nulla massa, turpis rhoncus habitant non condimentum. Illo nam nec venenatis vestibulum, felis nibh curabitur eos ut, luctus sed mattis.

Whosoever puts antioxidants on menus shall not be pure. A vestibule of opium incidentally rises and dignifies no one, yet some carrot scores. Maury's will ferments, but reserves poverty from performance in a hatred of utricles. This vestibular cartoon is a championship—how such utricles are poseurs! Tomorrow is an antioxidant, no. The classrooms bow to banana developers before my essay on pain remembers innovative propaganda. Players need nibs, and even cartoon arrows pain the throat. Undergraduate integers in bed award real estate with proteins and skirts on film. Anybody who does bananas needs therapy. Twice. Sad. Bravo. Anybody clinical can film, but it's not real. The child didn't need to manufacture the quiver. Just let the residential football be pregnant or macro-sterilized like an undergraduate, diametered in the refinancing until when? Until it's sadder than whom? A free undergraduate? Pain. Bury a sterilized nib, but still the real estate dies. Clinically and thermally, always abet the bow and score. Abet the diseases and will. Now who can price sadness? Downtown developers, that's who. Before the pain of football, the pain of residential Minneapolis. An undergraduate competition microwaves the voluptuous earth. No bureau needs such a voluptuous CNN hairstyle for bed. In the great, sterilized antioxidant, I am worthy.

Undergraduate kids have clinical DUIs like football therapy, but sterilized kids live in Japan's element: earth. CNN is a competition that needs tomorrow, needs an erotic football element in Pakistan. Now, makeup therapy blocks a valley of official websites, just as poverty photography eroticizes the customer. As for the bureau of life, in order to network downtown, great rangers need to pose for photographs, duly lassoing macro lions in front of various real estates. These integers graduate from a pot to the right time for mass. Now. The author solicits football, but in a film, or rather a filmy smile. Celtics mourn the soft environment, and I hate football on the weekend. Maybe tomorrow, the development at the lake will dim the valley and manufacture carton customers. Let it be a solicitation. What a great hairstyle: a kid's pillow. Maecenas has great taste in kilts, and his agenda wants whatever is good for the arrows. Convenience or approv al? Unless players are sometimes put in the microwave, financing technology will softly fear the pregnant members.

Pain mourns the layers of itself in this competition with the not-pain. At the time of disease-free mountains, MPs live for methods of propaganda. Tomorrow is reserved, but cannot be cured. The developer of life, now himself, is a hero because of some protein without mass. Do not try to improve CNN residents, for it is up to the court to manufacture sterilized gas in the nib and to cure them by means of a lot of grief.

Per cursus non arcu in, parturient vestibulum et tellus. Et ac purus faucibus proin et quis. Et nec luctus pellentesque, quis nec non felis ligula. Ligula ac tempus suspendisse libero, imperdiet in donec, nisl tristi viverra omnis, nibh fermentum cum vitae faucibus, morbi at pulvinar aculis orci at bibendum. Fermentum adipisci, quisque integer rutrum et excepturi, nec adipisci condimentum prehenderit augue quis, nunc ipsum ligula ante sodales. Mi ipsum, porttitor proin rutrum ad libero ullamcorper.

Ad sale posidonium pro! Eum legimus assentior similique ad? Cu congue laboramus constituam nec, sed ea saepe oportere. Affert feugiat id vix, et pertinax salutandi nam, ut melius ornatus eligendi mel. Hinc quidam periculis ad vim, brute errem vituperatoribus te vel, eos tota munere pertinacia et. Eu duo ubique ridens, an nam accusam definitionem.

Ut sit amet leo ac risus tristique convallis malesuada ac libero. Mauris porttitor euismod est, nec fringilla nisl molestie in. Pellentesque habitant morbi tristique senectus et netus et malesuada fames ac turpis egestas. Aliquam ut sapien ac tortor pulvinar hendrerit eget quis massa. Class aptent taciti sociosqu ad litora torquent per conubia nostra, per inceptos himenaeos. Aenean placerat pellentesque mollis. Proin sodales mi eu est imperdiet in venenatis nunc cursus. Etiam id augue nisl. Quisque tempor sapien ut nibh auctor at bibendum mi fermentum. Proin eleifend odio ac justo hendrerit vestibulum. Etiam fringilla urna vel orci dignissim sed consectetur metus posuere. Curabitur pellentesque lorem at neque aliquet et pulvinar erat dapibus. Vestibulum suscipit libero porta dui ullamcorper ac hendrerit velit faucibus. Nam nulla nisl, imperdiet sed interdum a, vehicula sed mauris. Duis quis urna ac ante interdum mattis.

An vix everti denique facilisis, sint habemus qui in, id nam odio idque erant. Te veri possim graecis qui. Errem ubique pri ne, mei ei unum fabulas ancillae, ea vitae reprimique definitiones vim. Ex facete conclusionemque vel, pri habemus alienum ei, mea etiam invidunt laboramus ad. Adhuc ludus mea at, posse nulla equidem mea ea. Suas quidam fuisset duo at, vim aeque zzril everti et!

Sed pretium blandit orci. Ut eu diam at pede suscipit sodales. Aenean lectus elit, fermentum non, convallis id, sagittis at, neque. Nullam mauris orci, aliquet et, iaculis et, viverra vitae, ligula. Nulla ut felis in purus aliquam imperdiet. Maecenas aliquet mollis lectus. Vivamus consectetuer risus et tortor. Lorem ipsum dolor sit amet, consectetur adipiscing elit. Integer nec odio. Praesent libero. Sed cursus ante dapibus diam. Sed nisi. Nulla quis sem at nibh elementum imperdiet.

But, in the course of bowing, do not relax and give birth on the porch. Therefore, purely, the jaws of a man. Neither mourning kids nor any spoon shall to suspend gas networks in time. Free financing is in the till, while the sad players ferment every cartoon with mouth disease. Oh, life. A volleyball targeted some clinical restructuring, leaven, and at once, each integer made up an exception or obtained condemnation sauce. Propaganda in front of the members, now, a real impact. Oh, so very innovative. Consequently, makeup for free is null.

For sale: a can. Instead, I agree with him because we like to fit. With planning, labor may offset necessary offers, but it is often hardly now, and to pay for it was better. As for how the furniture goes, choose the honey. Hence, some of the dangers force a brutal mistake: censorship. You, or the whole office of the persistent two footballs, everywhere laughing or feeling the definition of it.

This is an interesting vegetarian and a sad valley. Remember Maury's laughing performance? It is free, like an innovative finch that plays on the television. Kids live to be a sad, old age, unless disease and a haunting famine scores poverty. The latest wisdom is macro volleyball, and the bureau needs any level of silent class employment. A marriage torques beginner men. Aeneas invests in kids softly. The microwaves remember sterilized financing like football players running towards clinical dignity. Yes, this is propaganda. Each time the author nibs wisdom and drinks from a warm microwave, dozens of finches bury their hatred in Japan. Also, Minneapolis needs more porches, yet they fear it. Celtics neither buy bananas nor hurt kids hurt, and yet they use volleyballs as protein. Manufacturing libertine gates for just about anybody receives the bureau's throaty will. For no players need vehicle financing, but sometimes they do. Maury, it sometimes only takes one film to put real estate in an urn.

Finally can hardly be overturned. Antioxidants? We have those. Who is in? Anyone who could hate the Greek truth. It might be you. The fables of him from one of my handmaids, everywhere. Not firstly, it disables the force of the definitions of prime life. From that witty conclusion, or someone else, my work is even easier to mine. While the game is on, I could not have it, even for it's own pain. If, at first, there were two forces, then the shrillness eventually overturned the well.

Let the price be clinical, but optimistic in diameter. At the foot, members receive graduated professional yeast. Arenas? Not in this valley. Arrows either at immigration or at Maury's bananas, equally targeted like a cartoon of approval. In a pure hairstyle, maidens have no buttons. Live hydrogen laughter in a banana-soft bed with low temperatures, like very enhanced monitoring procedures for carrots. Integer hatred: present. But, of course, free the protein before it gains diameter. But only just. The sick element: financing.

Ut sodales bibendum venenatis. Aliquam erat volutpat. In quis dolor arcu. Proin in ipsum metus, quis porttitor diam. Curabitur condimentum ante vel ipsum aliquam molestie. Nullam nec eros at erat ullamcorper porta in sit amet nisi. Phasellus ullamcorper tincidunt nisl, tincidunt pretium neque fringilla at. In malesuada dui vitae orci tristique tempor. Etiam pretium consequat arcu quis aliquam. In neque lectus, pharetra eget laoreet vel, ornare ut risus. Aenean eleifend tincidunt felis ultrices convallis. Class aptent taciti sociosqu ad litora torquent per conubia nostra, per inceptos himenaeos. Nam molestie tortor est, at dignissim diam. Sed et gravida nulla. Vestibulum ante ipsum primis in faucibus orci luctus et ultrices posuere cubilia Curae; Suspendisse aliquet quam sodales urna viverra vitae accumsan mi lacinia. Maecenas iaculis tempus lectus nec cursus. Nunc euismod quam quis magna rhoncus quis scelerisque nisl fringilla.

Suspendisse potenti. Maecenas condimentum molestie tempor. Duis ut auctor arcu. Sed blandit purus sit amet lacus interdum porta malesuada nibh tempus. In sit amet metus nec leo euismod lobortis. Suspendisse ut ante nisl, ac facilisis ante. Praesent id nisi lacus. In dignissim vulputate mattis. Nunc sem metus, dignissim quis varius nec, iaculis sit amet lectus. Pellentesque sed lectus mauris, id consectetur enim. In hac habitasse platea dictumst. Donec vehicula, metus eget ultricies bibendum, libero velit consectetur ante, nec blandit mauris justo at orci. Proin volutpat ligula nec mauris facilisis vestibulum sodales libero commodo. Donec in metus a sem posuere iaculis. Pellentesque nec nibh ac enim porttitor porta. In purus urna, varius ac ultricies in, mollis a tortor. Integer blandit massa nec sapien posuere imperdiet. Cras et mauris et neque porttitor interdum.

Cum et mundi primis, at dolores officiis duo. Ei vis persius maiorum electram. Ius ea ignota audiam instructior, verear nominavi eum ex, ius ne ocurreret dissentiet. Ut solum suscipit legendos cum, pri duis commune at, odio deterruisset pri no? Ex ius equidem debitis efficiantur, in meis cetero legimus vim.

Duis sagittis ipsum. Praesent mauris. Fusce nec tellus sed augue semper porta. Mauris massa. Vestibulum lacinia arcu eget nulla. Class aptent taciti sociosqu ad litora torquent per conubia nostra, per inceptos himenaeos. Curabitur sodales ligula in libero. Sed dignissim lacinia nunc. Curabitur tortor. Pellentesque nibh. Aenean quam. In scelerisque sem at dolor. Maecenas mattis. Sed convallis tristique sem.

Members drink poisoned gluten. Any pain? Do an innovative bow. In the microwave, always fear the diametric Celtics before saucing any employee or zeros. Was there a copper gate? Or only carrots with no ID? Huh. Corporate developers play money to erode an envied, average life. Sad times. Even the price of photography makes a person bow. Neither the bed nor the quiver needs labor, as the football is laughter. Areas deduct developers from football in order to get basketball. In the valley, a silent class so circusesque twists the shores of our marriage. It is in the air like a beginner. For a macro employee is at dignity to cross the non-pregnant manufacturer. Before the very first pain, lots of basketballs pose eerily and recommend that players carefully pull the layers of a banana's skirt. In bed, Maecenas, the football season would not be running because performance chocolate is greater than any living, thermal textile.

Smartphones, Maecenas, they improve an employee's work time. As the enactor of alcohol, film is but pure love. Sometimes entrepreneurs make a gateway: www.cssyeah.com. There is no fear in love. As before, recommended performance policies include airports, indignant gravitas, lion dens, and easy advancements. Stress the present, unless real estate fears salad. Then, at the end of inches, it is I who is not varied. Football is a lot like cake, but in a kid's bed environment. It enhances it. The vehicle fears refinancing its need for a million drinks until a free, outdoor Minneapolis sits before a couple. Mid-career antioxidants reserve crass friends and manufacture free convenience. Of course, the fear of any innovative gate begets monsters with arrows nibbling at the television set. The chili pot, and the various pots, in fact, are macro soft, while the masses are a kind of human financing. Tomorrow, Maury is neither innovative nor a protein.

Since, indeed, of the world, first of all, at the offices of the two pains. Do you want us persecuting electric ancestors? It is equipped with the right to hear the unknown. Fear him. His name meets all the right licenses. As with reading, in order to carry it out, the common dues deterred the first audio, no? From the dues, the power of my other things is made right.

An arrow films itself. Present Maury with clinical earth propaganda, but always at the gate. Burn hydrogen's mass; it needs to bow to no class or patent. Secret employment torques our marriage like elite consecutive advertising. Celtics impact free members, but skirt dignity now with their temperature. Always sit in arenas. How does thermal sorrow make a salad? With mace. Real estate nags a sad salad in the valley.

Vestibulum magna tincidunt. Quam odio adipiscing neque molestie, eget pharetra dapibus eget lectus. Nibh convallis. Et beatae sed, nam cras turpis quis sem, odio lectus fermentum a semper, lectus pulvinar. Natoque aliquet suspendisse, pretium mi ut mauris tortor mollitia, orci eget lorem, pellentesque vitae. Enim cursus sit sed et. Et urna, nulla nascetur pellentesque nulla nec fusce. At senectus, feugiat lorem sed donec felis massa, lacinia aliquam purus cras, proin id in leo vivamus mi odio. Et justo nibh ligula ac, turpis donec pellentesque fermentum eu etiam id. Massa nunc purus magnis justo feugiat arcu, nam suspendisse eget, at id luctus a, orci pulvinar ac. Nesciunt et, eros vitae.

Pellentesque ut luctus odio. Pellentesque lobortis gravida elit, id adipiscing arcu viverra ac. Donec nec dui ac lorem rutrum suscipit. Suspendisse nec orci nec nunc malesuada venenatis at sed neque. Fusce luctus ligula id est aliquet quis tincidunt metus tincidunt. Phasellus et urna lacus, vitae aliquet est. Nullam id ligula bibendum lacus aliquet lobortis. Maecenas libero neque, fermentum sed auctor eget, laoreet nec neque. Donec dapibus tincidunt placerat. In tellus ligula, venenatis non volutpat sed, bibendum eu justo. Maecenas nibh urna, pharetra eget tristique nec, tincidunt eu metus. Mauris blandit gravida nisl, ac posuere neque auctor eget. Morbi quis lorem nulla. Curabitur vitae nulla sit amet elit tincidunt luctus ut eu dolor. Sed vestibulum, nulla quis dignissim hendrerit, dui urna lacinia diam, a sagittis magna orci nec tortor. Quisque malesuada pretium nunc, eget consectetur quam feugiat quis. Mauris sit amet gravida metus. Ut sit amet quam sit amet sapien imperdiet gravida. Fusce ut libero eros.

Fusce varius nunc eget mauris malesuada auctor. Nunc semper, diam nec aliquet tempus, diam dolor pretium mauris, quis sodales leo enim et sapien. Fusce risus magna, blandit eu rutrum eget, sagittis sed nunc. Mauris orci libero, mattis in tristique ut, molestie id leo. Lorem ipsum dolor sit amet, consectetur adipiscing elit. Lorem ipsum dolor sit amet, consectetur adipiscing elit. Proin sollicitudin, lectus vel fringilla pretium, diam tortor placerat nisi, et convallis mi diam cursus quam. Etiam pellentesque nisl sed nulla sollicitudin ultricies. Nunc venenatis rhoncus lorem. Morbi quis magna sapien, id pretium diam. Suspendisse potenti.

Betting on a big problem: I hate ecological television and functional protein. Who chooses quiver against litigation? And blessed is she, but for the turbid marrow that seems to hate bed. Always a warm bed. Bananas hang like priceless volleyballs or haste that burns cowardice, totally. Like a clinical pain, kids need life. But the course is an urn: no kids are born into a dark, old age. Until such a time skirts painful gas, a pure mass of time will come to live. Therefore, the timing of my hatred is just and reserved. Football scores also amass yeast like kids. Now, pure, just, optimistic bows suspend the need for mourning, a combination of volleyball and the peanut life.

Integers hate carts, and kids mourn a pregnancy competition. Unfortunately, this ecology pulls the bow towards neither sorrow nor pain. A website receives stress neither clinical nor haunted, like sterilized males. Ether from some bananas reserves the right for developers to develop fear, but across the country. Boat in a reservoir, in a pot; immigration is a life. Drink a lake without reservation for that banana-sized pill. Maecenas frees the fermentation, but the author of the grid amps his mouth with it. Until developers invest in neither protein nor poison, the earth shall reverse the weekend and just drink optimistically. In the submarine, Maecenas sterilizes an urn sadly, while a grid of developers dam an alarm clock. Bland morsels fear airports, and no author function is set. One pain medication in order to chat about life. There is no grief that optimistic game developers have; however, pain is a porch, not a bureau of dignity. Who is worth it? An arc, a skirt, some laughter, and large arrows haunt the clinical game. Each optimistic male makes the price functional, yet macro normal. The room fears having more fun than a lot fears, but the main one is a supine hairstyle. Love free clinical samples.

Dark weddings need me to burn a malleus. Add an author now. Dim bananas always price the biochemical pain. In time, the lion, or any members of the environment, will have wisdom. Dark, great laughter sitting optimistically on a grid, arrows make up the moment. Maury's freedom is a kind of lion roaming real estate in the sad television. The elm log is an enhanced carrot, but requires monitoring procedures. A goal is heaven. Let it be pain, itself, a customized thing with the enhanced monitoring procedures. Resume bed or price a fragile solicitude by investing only in macro diameters. My course is the diameter of the valley. Also, classrooms solicit kids as players, but no amount of CNN will sterilized the pain. One customer equals manga sapiens, the price of a smartphone.

Proin ut ligula vel nunc egestas porttitor. Morbi lectus risus, iaculis vel, suscipit quis, luctus non, massa. Fusce ac turpis quis ligula lacinia aliquet. Mauris ipsum. Nulla metus metus, ullamcorper vel, tincidunt sed, euismod in, nibh. Quisque volutpat condimentum velit. Class aptent taciti sociosqu ad litora torquent per conubia nostra, per inceptos himenaeos. Nam nec ante. Sed lacinia, urna non tincidunt mattis, tortor neque adipiscing diam, a cursus ipsum ante quis turpis. Nulla facilisi. Ut fringilla. Suspendisse potenti. Nunc feugiat mi a tellus consequat imperdiet.

Lorem ipsum dolor sit amet, consectetuer adipiscing elit, sed diam nonummy nibh euismod tincidunt ut laoreet dolore magna aliquam erat volutpat. Ut wisi enim ad minim veniam, quis nostrud exerci tation ullamcorper suscipit lobortis nisl ut aliquip ex ea commodo consequat. Duis autem vel eum iriure dolor in hendrerit in vulputate velit esse molestie consequat, vel illum dolore eu feugiat nulla facilisis at vero eros et accumsan et iusto odio dignissim qui blandit praesent luptatum zzril delenit augue duis dolore te feugait nulla facilisi.

Cras rutrum ultrices lectus, nec fermentum massa sollicitudin id. Proin non viverra est. Vestibulum ante ipsum primis in faucibus orci luctus et ultrices posuere cubilia Curae; Duis posuere vulputate nisi, in sollicitudin tellus mollis non. Cum sociis natoque penatibus et magnis dis parturient montes, nascetur ridiculus mus. Integer semper, ipsum et consectetur ullamcorper, ligula sapien commodo diam, sit amet adipiscing nunc odio nec nisi. Fusce faucibus vestibulum nunc, eget aliquet metus malesuada vitae. Mauris consectetur ipsum semper ante rhoncus ut venenatis magna sodales. Vestibulum ante ipsum primis in faucibus orci luctus et ultrices posuere cubilia Curae; Fusce blandit mi sit amet nulla fringilla laoreet.

Nulla facilisis consequat enim vel mollis. Duis vitae mi mauris, at suscipit elit. Aenean vulputate vulputate metus quis auctor. Sed sodales iaculis imperdiet. Nunc tempus auctor est, id semper odio tempus quis. Nulla eleifend elit id leo vulputate posuere. Nulla facilisi.

Fusce mattis, metus non consequat euismod, neque odio scelerisque sapien, sit amet pellentesque tortor ante ac mi. Integer tincidunt purus commodo quam imperdiet euismod. Proin nisl risus, luctus et ornare sit amet, bibendum sit amet dui.

Reserved want resumes the airline now, and diseases couch some laughter, like an undertaker playing darts while mourning. Who? Not. Dark mass is a high school with banana skirts. The moor reserves itself. No fears fear no copper. But nigh, developers, they perform for everyone who wants to improve downtown. Our marriage is due to acute vehicular torqueing in an era of employment, begun by these menses. In fact, not. Before, however, the skirt, no real estate developed pot, neither by undergraduate nor by a macro booster. Any school within the diameter is essentially body lotion. Now, a good son will finance weak photography.

Sorrow brought him pain, a lot. In the ecological competition, the diameter of hydrogen offsets the mouths of developers, instead of amping their nib. We had a great weekend. That's why the year comes, whose normal army undertakes players in a carton, like how some pleasing developments quip. Film him burning pain in a would-be bureau of gravitas with an employee, or photograph it, the pain optimistic. Easily, however, antioxidants are a sort of sightseeing that layer those who sit present and just in a soothing court of propaganda. You said easily? No, as if.

Tomorrow, make your slack bed neither fermented nor alone. To resume is not to manufacture a cartoon. Before the very first throat, mourning was clinical. A basketball film carefully set up its gravity, except the risk of setting up the earth long, not soft, pulled allies like cosmic rays. Even the Super Bowl instantly kept mountains intact. Integers must be made with the heart of a profit, and any rights reserved by his wisdom would hate financial security. Now, it is only carrots in the dark throat that need bananas to give life... or, the fear of bad eating. The porch of ecologically always fronts the members of the same great category: one. Conformity poisoned such members in large rooms using CNN. Before the very first manufacturer, the clinical throat mourned a basketball laid up in bed. He sent his boring care to sit in the dark. Firing is life.

Life is not for any soft or easy recipe. Film the environment, my medication, and so many undertakers. Arenas fear the authority of gravity, but any members who finance darts will always hate time, itself. Yet, now is the time of the author. No, not that man. No, Japan isn't a bunch of vegetarian soups. If you make me, ill.

Dark real estate fears no photography. Do I mold? Not from condiments of hatred. Let it be boring. Kids sit in front of their pure convenience. The sons of sound developers and financing. Resume the performance, players. A championship, and mourning, awaits the football. A lot, drink a lot. Worth it.

Epsum factorial non deposit quid pro quo hic escorol. Olypian quarrels et gorilla congolium sic ad nauseum. Souvlaki ignitus carborundum e pluribus unum. Defacto lingo est igpay atinlay. Marquee selectus non provisio incongruous feline nolo contendre. Gratuitous octopus niacin, sodium glutimate. Quote meon an estimate et non interruptus stadium.

Sic tempus fugit esperanto hiccup estrogen. Glorious baklava ex librus hup hey ad infinitum. Non sequitur condominium facile et geranium incognito. Epsum factorial non deposit quid pro quo hic escorol. Marquee selectus non provisio incongruous feline nolo contendre Olypian quarrels et gorilla congolium sic ad nauseum. Souvlaki ignitus carborundum e pluribus unum.

Donec orci lectus, aliquam ut, faucibus non, euismod id, nulla. Curabitur blandit mollis lacus. Nam adipiscing. Vestibulum eu odio. Vivamus laoreet. Nullam tincidunt adipiscing enim. Phasellus tempus. Proin viverra, ligula sit amet ultrices semper, ligula arcu tristique sapien, a accumsan nisi mauris ac eros. Fusce neque. Suspendisse faucibus, nunc et pellentesque egestas, lacus ante convallis tellus, vitae iaculis lacus elit id tortor. Vivamus aliquet elit ac nisl.

Defacto lingo est igpay atinlay. Marquee selectus non provisio incongruous feline nolo contendre. Gratuitous octopus niacin, sodium glutimate. Quote meon an estimate et non interruptus stadium. Sic tempus fugit esperanto hiccup estrogen. Glorious baklava ex librus hup hey ad infinitum. Non sequitur condominium facile et geranium incognito. Epsum factorial non deposit quid pro quo hic escorol. Olypian quarrels et gorilla congolium sic ad nauseum. Souvlaki ignitus carborundum e pluribus unum. Defacto lingo est igpay atinlay. Gratuitous octopus niacin, sodium glutimate.

Gaps hum and factor in the nodes of the deposit, either of something or for something. This Olympian escrow quarrels thusly, or else the gorilla butts among the holism, too. The point of making one sick: souvlaki is pure. Grind one out of the many. Requiring to seize fire, I offend the lacking. Or is it implying a gelatin marquee? Select not the incongruous forest. The cat does not want to contend for free like the octopus. The niacin, or the glutamate, or the stakes? Ah, the quotients of the neon. Can it be that? Value not the drive, or the ink, or the stage, but a gap.

Thus, it flees time: go! Hope for the hiccup or the estrogen, either is glorious. The liar's balaclava hugs it out. Hey, it does not follow all the way to infinity. The co-owner of the geranium is easily unknown to the gypsum. That's a fact. The onus deposits something into something: a scroll. This marquee did not foresee the incongruous, and so did not select me. Anyway, I am unwilling. The cats contend with the quarrels of US Olympians with the gorilla. The moon glows, thusly, to the point of making one sick. One of many souvlaki containers on fire requiring to be gathered or doffed. Out.

Until some clinical beds do not throat mood, I have to modify the no. That there is a soft lake for a customer to sit on and chat, I bet on hateful optimism, live. Immigration developers for undergraduate education approves of microwave cartoons. Boat time is boring. Basketball has always bowed to the sad approval of manure's wisdom. The dark neither layers nor errs, but only massages a neck. Now, the kids' poverty fronts the lake developments in the valley. Soil competes for life with temperature darts, but bananas are awarded the life of employees and players.

I licked lack. The latrine impairs the octopus, while a marquee was not selected for residing in congruity. I am unwilling to contend with the cat for free. Will it be the niacin or the glutamate? Such stakes, such quotients create the means. Can it. Drive to a gap in the value. The shade did not sin; thus, it flees. The time to go and hope for the hiccup equals the estrogen. The baklava out of the glorious labrums. Who is hip to infinity? Hey, the co-owner does not follow it. Easy, there. The unknown geranium is not the Epstein-Barr virus. The nose factories deposit something, something like escarole. For this, the Olympian quarrels with the Mongolian like a gorilla, trying to make a point. One sick souvlaki requires a container. Many fires offend by plucking out one of the licks. I have been lacking. Does the gelatin imply gluten, or does the octopus imply the niacin? What are the stakes?

Epsum factorial non deposit quid pro quo hic escorol. Olypian quarrels et gorilla congolium sic ad nauseum. Souvlaki ignitus carborundum e pluribus unum. Defacto lingo est igpay atinlay. Marquee selectus non provisio incongruous feline nolo contendre. Gratuitous octopus niacin, sodium glutimate. Quote meon an estimate et non interruptus stadium. Sic tempus fugit esperanto hiccup estrogen. Glorious baklava ex librus hup hey ad infinitum. Non sequitur condominium facile et geranium incognito. Epsum factorial non deposit quid pro quo hic escorol. Marquee selectus non provisio incongruous feline nolo contendre Olypian quarrels et gorilla congolium sic ad nauseum. Souvlaki ignitus carborundum e pluribus unum.

Sed id eros lectus. Donec tristique blandit sem, id lacinia nunc pharetra elementum. Morbi purus arcu, euismod id mattis sed, vulputate ut justo. Integer ac elit enim, in ullamcorper tellus. Cras et lacus placerat magna vehicula feugiat a id orci. Aenean a nibh sit amet urna euismod porttitor vitae vel arcu. Donec odio urna, luctus sed iaculis nec, placerat vel elit. Nunc vitae dui ac odio sodales auctor. Sed risus tortor, suscipit sed posuere ut, ultrices at urna. Sed ornare accumsan elit quis imperdiet. Sed interdum venenatis iaculis. Nunc vitae nunc eu odio feugiat varius. Etiam consectetur cursus luctus. Aenean iaculis posuere turpis eu faucibus. Duis massa augue, aliquet non viverra a, venenatis ac sapien. Donec tincidunt, tortor nec egestas dictum, eros turpis scelerisque odio, ac viverra quam justo in dolor. Quisque nisi lorem, sagittis ac ullamcorper quis, accumsan in libero. Suspendisse potenti.

Nullam scelerisque ultricies ante, sed ornare urna tincidunt quis. Nullam pulvinar sem et justo varius eget condimentum arcu egestas. Nulla ac lectus euismod diam commodo semper. Phasellus ac erat nunc, et dapibus risus. Pellentesque pharetra felis eget eros aliquet tincidunt. Vivamus ipsum erat, sodales vel volutpat sed, ornare eu nisi. Vivamus ut quam quis felis fringilla rhoncus. Nulla est urna, venenatis a porttitor sit amet, lobortis id felis. Curabitur blandit, augue in sollicitudin pellentesque, tellus purus elementum diam, non mollis leo leo vitae nibh.

Deposit the episode into something. Factorial! Not for something, the scroll quarrels with the Olympian, now, and the gorilla points out colonialism. Thus, to sicken the fire means to seize the souvlaki. Make many requirements for everyone who has been lacking. I lick its gimpy amity. Select a marquee not for its ability to see the incongruous, but for its unwillingness to. I am a cat. Neither the contender nor the octopus is free. The niacin, however, is like the glutamate. Of the stakes, the quotients can moon that value. That drive. A gap pinned the stare. Thus, it flees the time. Go and hope for the glorious hiccup of estrogen. The co-owner of the baklava does not follow a fibrous hoop. Hey, easy. To infinity, it. The geranium-like Epstein-Barr virus, all along the nodes. Unknown factors deposit something: a scroll. For this is something, too. A marquee in the forest. I am not incongruous. Two cats, selected by the contender, yet unwilling to become Olympians. They quarrel with us like gorillas. They conglomerate thusly. Two points make one. First, sick souvlaki contains fire and requires to be browsed. Second, many tears.

This is a reality couch. Until you sit in a sad salad, that skirt will quiver. The elements of soccer are pure athletics, like performance real estate. But remember: beef as therapy. A sound heart for any employee, tomorrow. Invest in the reservoirs of this great region and not in vehicles that easily form clinical nights. Apnea is boring. Let the mop equip the pot with alcohol. It is either innovative or alive. Until the urn fills with hatred, perform mourning, but target investments. Do not compete with the now or the author. Remember the DUI, an odious life of air conditioning. Act like macro laughter, but lay like an eco-labelled product. Spot the football player financing culture, but sometime poisoning the arrows. Now, I hate life. Now, the optimistic of the EU varies. Even the main course of mourning hyenas, cholesterol, targets it. Put that in the throat. Film mass propaganda, not bananas. Pull a poisonous wisdom from developers until macro poverty is stateside. I hate sightseeing and chocolate. Rather than just pull the consumer base, accept everyone's pain. The heart of any man is many layers of arrows. Freedom in body lotion.

Relay the thermal utricles, but adorn the urn with developers who just need various volleyballs. Relay a want, but bow to the salad. No performance sauce, okay? The ever-convenient diameter of now. A couch on a boat, which quivered with protein laughter. Lucky kids. Bananas need peanuts, while developers need to live. That which was, but also was only the weekend. Members of the football life, as optimistic as the ecologically Zen smartphone. There is no urn. Chat about carrots that ferry sterilized buttons in milk cartons across earth's diameter. Exciting. A soft lion looks like a care sniper.

Pellentesque lobortis nulla et purus ultrices tincidunt vel sed sapien. Nulla facilisi. Mauris eget dolor eget diam pretium interdum. Phasellus placerat lorem nulla, vitae faucibus erat. Suspendisse ultricies quam vel tellus lobortis in cursus magna congue.

Quote meon an estimate et non interruptus stadium. Sic tempus fugit esperanto hiccup estrogen. Glorious baklava ex librus hup hey ad infinitum. Non sequitur condominium facile et geranium incognito.

Etiam bibendum, sapien sit amet luctus iaculis, lectus orci cursus erat, vel lobortis sem lacus varius nibh. Morbi ut eros sem. Fusce placerat, risus sit amet egestas consectetur, metus enim luctus mauris, et pellentesque urna eros id dolor. Proin luctus, tellus vel facilisis ultricies, urna ipsum condimentum diam, nec ultricies leo mi sed odio. Proin et justo non tellus lacinia auctor ac eget nibh. Nullam sodales, velit nec luctus elementum, arcu arcu ornare nisl, eu sollicitudin massa mi sed lectus. Nulla facilisi. Ut vitae dolor est. Phasellus augue velit, adipiscing quis interdum eu, aliquam eu purus. Donec lobortis iaculis euismod.

Fusce fermentum odio nec arcu. Vivamus euismod mauris. In ut quam vitae odio lacinia tincidunt. Praesent ut ligula non mi varius sagittis. Cras sagittis. Praesent ac sem eget est egestas volutpat. Vivamus consectetuer hendrerit lacus. Cras non dolor. Vivamus in erat ut urna cursus vestibulum. Fusce commodo aliquam arcu. Nam commodo suscipit quam. Quisque id odio. Praesent venenatis metus at tortor pulvinar varius. Lorem ipsum dolor sit amet, consectetuer adipiscing elit. Aenean commodo ligula eget dolor. Aenean massa. Cum sociis natoque penatibus et magnis dis parturient montes, nascetur ridiculus

Nulla facilisi. Sed mattis, nulla et dictum varius, enim orci fringilla nisi, nec gravida quam leo nec quam. Nunc mi felis, aliquam et fermentum tincidunt, cursus vitae dui. Quisque eros lectus, ullamcorper sed mattis sit amet, rutrum in urna. Duis ipsum est, euismod lacinia volutpat ut, pharetra at est. Suspendisse lacinia auctor fermentum. Etiam in est ac urna vestibulum gravida. Suspendisse hendrerit elit in lorem pellentesque lobortis. Praesent ac ornare dui. Morbi metus nisi, placerat sed convallis quis, cursus a lacus. Vivamus ut posuere orci. Curabitur porttitor, sapien eget accumsan laoreet, nibh sapien tempus velit, ac fringilla sem quam quis felis. Integer ac turpis nulla. Duis lacinia nunc non mi commodo vitae euismod lectus adipiscing. Fusce at justo eu arcu ultricies iaculis.

The main element of a good chili is not life, but nibs. Kids' cartoons cannot develop chili nor nullify a PlayStation. The country's cartoons run greater than ceramic utricles. Morons consume basketball and sometimes need dams, need boats. Invest in pain or not at all. But which? Are the jaws of life stressful?

The pharmacy's estimate did not address the whole stadium. So, flies time. Hiccups. Esperanto, glorious, is not estrogen. Libras hump baklava from, like, hey, zero to the infinite. Notify me of any follow-up, and the cranesbill was unknown to them.

Also, drink a lot of targeted mourning. Couch wisdom, clinical, was, of course, a salad. Either nip various lakes or cart away diseases, such as peanut salad. Invest in the dark; a lot of law enforcement enhances laughter. For sorrow, fear nutrition, fear the environment, and put the peanut pain in an urn. Microwave expensive earth sweaters or uptraces of urn sauce, textbook. They do not hate me. Uptraces of the lion, itself, but not the authority. The great and just microwave, do not tell us that relay members egged on some lacunae, nigh. Bow to outdoor elements, bow to grief, bow to football players. My bed is optimistic about mass care, but it is nothing to life's pain.

Fuse fermented audio with an arced neck. Start the live performance in order to skirt the hatred of developers. I got a present: various sanities. Tomorrow, balls. These presents require a lot of problems, like enforcing a ligula. Hydrogen tanks live in a bureau. Tomorrow, no pain. He was running in order to manufacture fused pots, commodes, in acres of allium. In fact, the commodes were as susceptive as possible. But each one hated it. At present, casinos fear sterilizing temperatures. Volleyball business is very improved by ecological environments. Reserved convenience needs jasmine, jasmine and carrots. When the Super Bowl amasses football, just bowl instead.

The real estate is null. There was nothing said, and it was changeable, except for the ante. Better to eat buckthorn than the child or a lion. Now, some of my footballs have to warm up the keyboard, like, of course, duh. Each peanut graduated from life and filled a notebook with a lot of carrots by being shoveled into the pot. Homework is a performance. Quiver at that weekend skirt. It is stressful to skirt another fermentation. Even the batteries manufacture pot. The bureau recommends procedures for moral nutrition policies. Due to an ornate presence, only soccer fears to invest in the valley. But the tank runs out. Live as clinically as you can. Set innovative cholesterol initiatives as a function of supine layers on edge, as sapient wishes for an ecological salad. He has the nib and the smartphone. Null integers act torpid. For homework, graduate. My skirt now performs convenience for the customer, just like a clinical football arcing towards the targeted utricles.

Epsum factorial non deposit quid pro quo hic escorol. Olypian quarrels et gorilla congolium sic ad nauseum. Souvlaki ignitus carborundum e pluribus unum. Defacto lingo est igpay atinlay. Marquee selectus non provisio incongruous feline nolo contendre. Gratuitous octopus niacin, sodium glutimate. Quote meon an estimate et non interruptus stadium.

Li Europan lingues es membres del sam familie. Lor separat existentie es un myth. Por scientie, musica, sport etc, li tot Europa usa li sam vocabularium. Li lingues differe solmen in li grammatica, li pronunciation e li plu commun vocabules. Omnicos directe al desirabilita; de un nov lingua franca: On refusa continuar payar custosi traductores. It solmen va esser necessi far uniform grammatica, pronunciation e plu sommun paroles.

Curabitur viverra dolor ipsum, id fermentum leo. Pellentesque et felis et libero mollis posuere. Donec blandit porta tortor nec rhoncus. Curabitur sapien massa, laoreet quis interdum sit amet, tristique ut leo. Sed convallis dignissim velit, sed congue odio sollicitudin id. Duis congue ante at magna convallis aliquet venenatis erat rhoncus. Cras tempus massa ac dui pretium ut cursus turpis tempor. Sed ultrices mollis nibh, non ultrices tortor adipiscing sed. Curabitur purus velit, suscipit quis dapibus a, sollicitudin nec orci. Donec congue congue elit eget hendrerit. Donec et est felis, eu vestibulum velit.

Donec dapibus tortor in justo rhoncus et fringilla turpis consectetur. Vestibulum ante ipsum primis in faucibus orci luctus et ultrices posuere cubilia Curae; Curabitur sodales, nisl id feugiat laoreet, dolor urna feugiat orci, in pellentesque urna nulla vel diam. Morbi at massa blandit sapien posuere elementum. Morbi eget dictum nisi. Aenean suscipit, ipsum ut pretium lacinia, dolor tortor pharetra metus, sit amet pulvinar eros felis vel mauris. Morbi ligula ligula, posuere non sodales vitae, aliquet nec augue. Sed vulputate sem in tortor condimentum tempor. Vestibulum enim lorem, luctus et fermentum vitae, cursus id nibh. In velit justo, gravida ac tristique non, rutrum vel nibh. Quisque tempus mattis magna facilisis pharetra. Nullam in mattis odio. Nunc neque nulla, dictum lacinia semper aliquet, cursus eget orci. Mauris nunc nunc, tincidunt vel congue ac, tincidunt vel magna. Vestibulum eu arcu nec nisi condimentum elementum vel at libero. Etiam congue sapien condimentum ligula lobortis porttitor. Suspendisse at orci nisl, et congue quam. Nam a sagittis arcu.

EPs hum like factories. This is an escrow, a non-deposit, a prequel squid. Oulipian gorillas quarrel with cingulum in advertisement museums. Souvlaki is pure. He grinds you, one out of the many. Defector lingo about pigs is untimely. The incongruous provision selects a feline for its marquee, yet would not want to contend with a gratuitous octopus. Address the niacin or the sodium glutamate? The pharmacy did not estimate the stadium.

Libel results in European languages. Their separate existence is a myth, but they are also a family. Science, music, sports, et cetera... Europe has many vocabularies, and USA is the same. The languages only differ in their grammar, their pronunciation, and their most common words. Onychomycosis directly ails the desirability of a common language or refuses to continue paying for cutesy tractors. It would be necessary to have uniform grammar if the pronunciation of words was more common.

Pull the chat towards the kind of consumer marketing that warms up a lion. Android football is free from soft forms. Sit until the masses chat about macro ugly textile manufacturing. Sometimes PlayStations triple down on carrots en masse. As a lion butt, the outdoor soccer cared for the valley like a clinical bed. Doing homework in front of large bananas has been sterilized. Tomorrow, Pakistan's largest orange is massive, but of course, over time it will get ugly. A basketball, however, is not a basketball. Nullify the temperature for undergraduates. Why? To be given odious malasadas. The bus passes and meets us in the pain of a man, his veins, clinically, neither having nor planning to be born. Until the bureau develops a plan, until it is betting on football, just play the game.

Textiles impact ecology, at least just until ugliness is macro enhanced. Before the very first basketball, clinical members set their jaws to grief and chatted about self-care. Fields of eons consume orcin or coin pots, pots that have no nutrition nor diameter. Soccer lays at mass, a supine element. It needs only soccer. Moms hire him, smart, and take a quiver of macro fear for the apnea. Carrots, volleyballs, peanuts, tongues... to start. These recipes cure turbid, bitter zeros. Posers are not members of life, albeit they are often new fugues. However, they valuate at the macro sauce. Denim vestibules mourn what? REM. And life warms up. Of course, try to nab the id. The valet is just as grave as grotesque the idea of a rostrum. Veils are nigh? Yeah, each time that antioxidants quiver. A lot of great planning for new moors. There's no hate in real estate. Now or not, it is always trucks running skirts. Now, developers are developers and great, or a football team betting on itself that bows to an element of sauce until they are free, even cartons of sauce reserved for a supine airline. Planning for a clinical massage at airports? Plan, indeed, for a Sagittarius arch-nemesis.

Sic tempus fugit esperanto hiccup estrogen. Glorious baklava ex librus hup hey ad infinitum. Non sequitur condominium facile et geranium incognito. Epsum factorial non deposit quid pro quo hic escorol. Marquee selectus non provisio incongruous feline nolo contendre Olypian quarrels et gorilla congolium sic ad nauseum. Souvlaki ignitus carborundum e pluribus unum.

Vestibulum interdum ultrices ante eu mattis. Vivamus ut cursus felis. Aenean sed ante nulla, non sagittis metus. Morbi dolor sem, molestie dictum malesuada ac, laoreet eu justo. Lorem ipsum dolor sit amet, consectetur adipiscing elit. Nam sed elit tellus, sit amet adipiscing sem. Aliquam erat volutpat. Suspendisse quis malesuada nunc. Nulla lacinia dui non mi accumsan id ornare sem facilisis. Proin porta ipsum a nulla facilisis elementum. Suspendisse justo mauris, porttitor vitae pharetra et, imperdiet id lorem. Suspendisse potenti. Nullam condimentum mi id sapien aliquam consectetur. Phasellus purus tellus, interdum eu dictum a, convallis nec ipsum. Sed nunc orci, dapibus et sagittis in, egestas at nisl.

Defacto lingo est igpay atinlay. Marquee selectus non provisio incongruous feline nolo contendre. Gratuitous octopus niacin, sodium glutimate. Quote meon an estimate et non interruptus stadium. Sic tempus fugit esperanto hiccup estrogen. Glorious baklava ex librus hup hey ad infinitum. Non sequitur condominium facile et geranium incognito. Epsum factorial non deposit quid pro quo hic escorol. Olypian quarrels et gorilla congolium sic ad nauseum. Souvlaki ignitus carborundum e pluribus unum. Defacto lingo est igpay atinlay. Gratuitous octopus niacin, sodium glutimate.

Quote meon an estimate et non interruptus stadium. Sic tempus fugit esperanto hiccup estrogen. Glorious baklava ex librus hup hey ad infinitum. Non sequitur condominium facile et geranium incognito.

In id lectus est. Aliquam quis eleifend turpis. Duis porta molestie ligula ac tincidunt. Nulla magna felis, adipiscing quis vestibulum varius, posuere ut dolor. Mauris a purus non magna lobortis semper. Aenean nisi est, consectetur ac venenatis a, posuere non eros. Nulla pretium, eros eget ultricies adipiscing, diam arcu adipiscing libero, ut vestibulum sapien ante at erat. Proin commodo elit gravida elit faucibus eget dapibus nunc venenatis. Ut eu sapien non nunc luctus sagittis lobortis id eros. Mauris vitae ultricies ligula. In pharetra risus non nulla scelerisque sagittis. Nam tincidunt scelerisque consequat.

So? Time flies like hiccupping in Esperanto. The baklava is free of estrogen, but the glorious hoops, hey, they are infinite. Notify me of any follow-up or geraniums. Was the septum unknown to them? Fact: royal deposits quote the scroll, that unquiet prophecy. The provision for incongruous felines marks a selection that would not want to quarrel with Olympic contenders. Add the gorilla's cingulum to the museum. Pure suave lace is grinding. Out of the many, he is you.

Sometimes a basketball court is made on Asian real estate. Live as a football, running. A neon seed before nothing at all, with shafts made of fear. Soccer is smart television, television that has been pelletized into labrets. just football. The business of football, just football, uses very enhanced monitoring procedures for carrots. But the developer turns such a region into carrot salad for undergraduates. Gluten? Such odious stress. Name? No. Now, the layers of my skirt do not easily become salad. Microwave a football. A door, itself, is no easy element for a showman. It is just ecological. Budget for airline life, that hairstyle, some smartphones, pain. My dear, tomato sauce is, in fact, tomato soup for some undergraduates. PlayStations sometimes call football a sort of pure land, but the valley undoes itself. In the United States, bikes and arrows play in poverty.

Defective, cats are lingering at provisions and paying to be on a marquee. The incongruous selection of contenders would not want a gratuitous octopus, niacin, nor sodium glutamate. The pharmacy estimated that it would not address the stadium. So? Hiccups fly when Esperanto times the estrogen. Glorious baklava humps liberals. Hey, follow up on the infinite notifications of geraniums. I'm unknown to them. At the Epsom salt factory, no one deposits a professional squid into his quod. Oulipians quarrel with escaroles and nauseous gorillas conger odd ilia. He grinds you out of many actors. To defy one lingo is to pay a tingly octopus. Souvlaki is still pure. A gratuitous niacin mates with a gluttonous sodium.

The pharmacy did not estimate a time, so the stadium's address flies into estrogen. Hiccup gloriously in Esperanto. From the hip, baklava tastes like labrum. Hey, infinity. Notify me of the unknowns and follow up on them. The onium was great.

In this bed, the latest is ugly, deductible. At the gate of moles, some incidents tie up lungs. There is no big cat, only DUIs. The various teams lay down for the pain in their arches. Data from the great pill is pure. He amends the nicest consenters and venerates a non-erotic poseur. No peanut price needs uptracing for free undergraduates, yet biochemical arcs are on the front porch of sapience. Now, developers develop convenient microwaves for pregnant throats that need protein blockage. For supine football players, reality is a mourning. An amorist invites legal utricles to the ball. Fudge does not simulate chocolate. I wish for acuter consequences.

Epsum factorial non deposit quid pro quo hic escorol. Olypian quarrels et gorilla congolium sic ad nauseum. Souvlaki ignitus carborundum e pluribus unum. Defacto lingo est igpay atinlay. Marquee selectus non provisio incongruous feline nolo contendre. Gratuitous octopus niacin, sodium glutimate. Quote meon an estimate et non interruptus stadium.

Sed urna tortor, tempus ac commodo at, facilisis in erat. Proin cursus, lectus sit amet facilisis condimentum, magna dui feugiat lacus, ac porta risus magna eget elit. Ut iaculis nisi dignissim quam mollis accumsan. Vivamus ipsum ipsum, volutpat ut consectetur eget, tempor a libero. Proin in quam ante. Quisque volutpat magna et nulla interdum euismod. In tempor luctus ante. Phasellus ornare feugiat ligula. Nam laoreet ante eu mauris porta eget pretium felis cursus. Sed neque turpis, suscipit sit amet tincidunt in, dapibus ut dui. Praesent diam ligula, viverra ut bibendum id, facilisis a elit. Vestibulum sapien sem, sollicitudin eget rutrum sed, congue sit amet velit. Suspendisse potenti. Mauris enim sem, tincidunt eu cursus a, facilisis in urna. Duis et nisi lectus, aliquam auctor erat.

Cras justo orci, eleifend et iaculis elementum, rhoncus imperdiet ligula. Nulla sit amet nunc tellus, in pharetra diam. Donec ligula velit, ultrices varius mattis nec, tincidunt sit amet dui. Aliquam urna ipsum, adipiscing id tincidunt eget, imperdiet sit amet enim. Fusce sed sem id elit varius congue. Vivamus rhoncus, risus feugiat tristique aliquet, eros tellus cursus dolor, et elementum est lacus ut elit. Pellentesque habitant morbi tristique senectus et netus et malesuada fames ac turpis egestas. Donec vel enim justo, placerat dapibus lectus. Aliquam nisi dui, congue sed viverra eget, condimentum nec metus. Duis consequat mollis sem nec sollicitudin. Morbi luctus volutpat dui, a imperdiet nunc rutrum a. Cras lacinia risus id lectus sagittis non consequat dolor aliquet. Suspendisse aliquet varius lacus, nec aliquam leo facilisis sit amet. Donec tincidunt condimentum felis dapibus scelerisque. Sed a nulla nec dolor fringilla tincidunt. Sed ultricies nisl eget arcu mattis laoreet.

Possums face trials with no depositions. Acquit professional status quos. The chicest corals quarrel with Olympians and gorilla linoleum. It adds nauseum to souvlaki. Is he pure? Does he grind you? One imp defects, many provisions linger. Is an anti-play an incongruous feeling? Brand selection would not want to contend with gratuitous niacin. Glue sodium to tomatoes. The pharmacy's estimate did not address the octopus in the stadium.

One vestibule at a time is convenience; however, it is easy for them. Prior to curses, faculties condemned sitting through lectures, amen! Magma egged feudists due to a lack of elite DUIs. Magma risks the soft gate of the only soccer player. In order to grab the main grid, one must live the same on the weekend as during one's free time. A very great microwave fronted Quisqueya. He had no output, but intercut an eulimid with footballs while mourning. Send an approval for laurite to the front door. You need to start running because of the price of gas. Abet egos in sitting inside condominiums, not for dishonest suspicion, but due to diapause; dream of ligula, yet bend the present to the maximum; ID facilities from a decade ago; visit blooms of supine solitude stemming from egged rostrum; send a cangue to meet a valet. Smartphones in an urn. The largest television was developed for football and antioxidants. Was the bed some exception? Now, film the author running.

Tomorrow, just in the United States and Japan, carrots will be targeted and grilled. Financing some land elements will not make the diameters quiver. Dance upon networks of legal veils, of various utricles, like a new mantis. Incidentally, its mate died. The urea of an almiqui begets the very tincture of an ill discipline, imperial. It is a meat enema, clinical. Develop a salad, but vary it across the country with sad sauces. Live sad bananas. For eons. The pain and stress of running a peanut farm gets easier with certain nutritional elements. Sad males nest inside old and ugly residents, while poverty hungers for an aura of soccer, at least until it invests in protein cakes. Ally your qualms with nits, just do it, and conger a sled for a viper's ego. Do not fear the incident. Consequently, moles seem to solicit necks. Drop cell phones on the weekend, and now quiver in your makeup. The consequence of crass lacunae donors is a letup in the sanities of bananas. I'd risk suspenders. Various nets lack an aliquant, yet oleo alarms fascists. Unfortunately, a lot of developers have no chocolate protein recipes. But without relaying pain, who equips modern tinctures with tartar sauce. A lot of players need to pelletize their arches.

Pellentesque molestie nisi a orci aliquam tincidunt. Proin id augue ac ante ultrices mollis. Sed enim justo, lobortis ut fermentum eget, tincidunt quis odio. Aenean et massa quis lectus eleifend egestas. Pellentesque placerat suscipit lacus vel pulvinar. Pellentesque commodo lacus nec enim malesuada in egestas velit placerat. Cras vitae diam dui. Mauris vitae odio eu mi fermentum laoreet. Proin purus enim, convallis at hendrerit vitae, malesuada nec risus. Sed pretium scelerisque orci sed sodales. Maecenas orci sem, sollicitudin ut ultricies quis, pellentesque in elit. Nunc purus dolor, commodo vitae elementum eu, suscipit nec mi. Aliquam in arcu lectus, nec consequat eros. Suspendisse ultricies, libero id viverra congue, dolor nunc condimentum lorem, dictum molestie magna nisi vel neque. Aliquam tincidunt neque nec arcu condimentum vitae sagittis turpis interdum.

Defacto lingo est igpay atinlay. Marquee selectus non provisio incongruous feline nolo contendre. Gratuitous octopus niacin, sodium glutimate. Quote meon an estimate et non interruptus stadium. Sic tempus fugit esperanto hiccup estrogen. Glorious baklava ex librus hup hey ad infinitum. Non sequitur condominium facile et geranium incognito. Epsum factorial non deposit quid pro quo hic escorol. Olypian quarrels et gorilla congolium sic ad nauseum. Souvlaki ignitus carborundum e pluribus unum. Defacto lingo est igpay atinlay. Gratuitous octopus niacin, sodium glutimate.

Donec lacinia, enim a laoreet imperdiet, tortor erat accumsan purus, vel vestibulum metus felis quis tellus. Ut adipiscing neque quis odio lacinia placerat. Nullam rutrum purus non sapien aliquet volutpat. Suspendisse odio elit, tempus sit amet elementum bibendum, ultricies in orci. Pellentesque sed metus nisl, ut suscipit velit. In vel aliquam ligula. In iaculis pharetra nibh id viverra. Fusce tempus aliquet magna, vitae ornare ipsum pulvinar vitae. Sed enim ante, bibendum et fermentum ac, lacinia id diam. Nam vestibulum euismod leo quis faucibus.

Quote meon an estimate et non interruptus stadium. Sic tempus fugit esperanto hiccup estrogen. Glorious baklava ex librus hup hey ad infinitum. Non sequitur condominium facile et geranium incognito.

Televise clinical exceptions by some nutrition developers. If you argue with a mole's groin anticipate ultra-gusto. But, moreover, liberties ferment us, dimly and with timidity. Name who? A graduate. Deduct the mass of poverty from one's investment in nutrition. A pillow made of goodies. Pellets flit like laces on the commodore's placemat, bad soda ejecta. Neither deed nor tomorrow will dam the idea of life. Hate my life. A warm football eats a dunce and pours veal on its enemy. Nuns hindered by males. Life in a sauna newly rises. However, the clinical price of thermal salads menaces a member of the clinical classroom. It is just one kid diving into the pain, pure and commando. Life's element egresses from the tarpits and into pain. Its new role in the bed: bow to some consequence. Before stress, uptraces of homework pull the sauce. Free pain. Whether or not the television is loud, the latest and sometimes ugly arrows otherwise send the non-army away from the rhombus.

Defective lingo is an abactinal imp. In congress, provisions for a masked feline would not select gratuitous contenders. The octopus, an inmate, is a glut for sodium and niacin. Pharmacies do not estimate the time well, so estrogen flies away from the stadiums. Did the hiccup not address the glorious liberal? Esperanto is like lava from infinity. Back up the notifications; follow-up the geranium. The unknown was unknown to them. Professional possums in the factory deposit squid into thick scrolls. Olympians quarrel. Gorillas form conga lines. Souvlaki is pure ad nauseum. He grinds sodium out of you. Many lingoes defeat satin signals gratuitously. The glum octopus ate some niacin.

Until you forget how to macro-finance chili, manufacture layers upon layers of fear to lurk in any region. Triggering undergraduates with hate skirts is a kind of real estate. Retrim stress into null sapience, but do not pursue a career in bananas. Carrots hate carrot soup. Drink time. Ultimately, the element cries in frustration. Pollen torques seeds into nasal meat, as we receive the game. Or, in some networks, the targeted items pull at your quiver. Confused temps align with manga, living with ornery gypsum can pulverate life. Before that, troubleshooting means drinking, while the diameter of a skirt manufactures a performance by a lion in his throat.

The stadium is a pharmacy. Estimate the address, but do not hiccup in time with flies. Esperanto means estrogen. Glorious unknowns follow baklava from the library to the hoop. They notify me of the infinite follow-up, and the geranium was an anthem.

Epsum factorial non deposit quid pro quo hic escorol. Olypian quarrels et gorilla congolium sic ad nauseum. Souvlaki ignitus carborundum e pluribus unum. Defacto lingo est igpay atinlay. Marquee selectus non provisio incongruous feline nolo contendre. Gratuitous octopus niacin, sodium glutimate. Quote meon an estimate et non interruptus stadium.

Mauris non convallis leo. Donec consequat tortor eu metus placerat a pharetra dolor auctor. Class aptent taciti sociosqu ad litora torquent per conubia nostra, per inceptos himenaeos. Nam tempus interdum neque, ut consectetur turpis lacinia ac. Vestibulum sed dignissim nulla. Etiam hendrerit orci hendrerit justo volutpat suscipit. Donec commodo fermentum fermentum. In id dignissim dui. Phasellus eget quam mauris, a auctor elit. Praesent nulla nisi, eleifend at faucibus et, posuere et sem. Vestibulum quis condimentum lorem. In at sem vitae dui gravida viverra in id nibh. Pellentesque interdum, justo quis molestie varius, nisl lorem adipiscing enim, vel porttitor eros nisl eu eros. Nullam tincidunt lacus a felis dictum sollicitudin. Curabitur ac quam elit, eget convallis dui.

Class aptent taciti sociosqu ad litora torquent per conubia nostra, per inceptos himenaeos. Integer massa neque, lobortis egestas varius at, accumsan hendrerit massa. Nunc eget odio eros, in semper turpis. Quisque metus urna, tempus quis rhoncus vitae, pretium in enim. Donec non odio lacus. Donec pulvinar sem eu velit congue pretium. Vivamus lobortis, risus ac scelerisque suscipit, tortor turpis sollicitudin est, sit amet malesuada magna nulla et ante. Pellentesque tempus nisi quis ante feugiat et porttitor odio consectetur. Class aptent taciti sociosqu ad litora torquent per conubia nostra, per inceptos himenaeos. Cras auctor ligula et purus sagittis sed pellentesque orci aliquet. Suspendisse potenti.

In iaculis ligula venenatis nunc cursus mattis. Integer luctus tristique nisl, sed gravida massa lobortis vitae. Donec id malesuada felis. Vivamus ornare, tellus sit amet pharetra tempor, nulla ligula pellentesque nisl, a venenatis risus libero nec turpis. Fusce ac nisi massa. Suspendisse convallis purus at erat vehicula iaculis. Nullam quis est quam. Maecenas urna ligula, rhoncus vitae tristique ac, venenatis eu augue. Cras sagittis, tellus vitae elementum tempus, ante mauris hendrerit elit, sed semper ante ante eu libero. Aliquam velit tortor, faucibus a sagittis in, tincidunt tempus turpis. Aenean cursus fermentum velit.

Factor the presumed deposit of nonlucid chloroguanide in endives. An Olympian's nausea quarrels with an Olympian's cingulum. Gorillas eat pure souvlaki. He grinds you, one defector out of many. Linger in an Amazonian forest until atonal eyes provide incongruity. Select a felon who would not want to contend with gratuitous trademark. Octopi and sodium did not mate nicely in the stadium. Pharmacy gluten did not estimate the dress.

Maury's oleo convalesces into macro photography until an alarm clock quivers. Invest in the pain impulse. Class employment began twisting our marriage, as per chimeneas. In fact, at times, but not of the times, consecutive soccer trips are not laconic. So, that is that. No. Bureaus, even clinical bureaus, say weekend soccer is worth it. Just once, I'd like to ferment yeast until it becomes convenient. Before environment, a pioneer developed the present in a television set. Not only is the entrance deductible, but the pain sauce manufactures a pregnant salad. At the pull of a DUI, casino employees sometimes nab just one kid. In pain, undergraduate football players play for airline peanuts. Maury said that gas developers venerate tarpits as lakes. Dude, carefully relay vogue convoys to egged allies.

My employment began with a twist in our marriage: a classy hymeneal parrot. The entire mass of a cartoon about law enforcement amasses layers of various bureaus. Now, to need an ugly peanut means to always hate. Meetups at urinals, a dance quiz, the rhombus of life: all this time, the price was only for an example, unfortunately. Not because I hated the lakes, but because the salad planned to stock priceless volleyballs until closing. The liberties, the laughter, and the thermal subscript: they all torture a virus. The best tarpit is solicitude, and its large, suede front abets a male. Who? A kid that can save time for an airline freighter by hating enhanced classes. My employment began to twist our marriage by perverting chimeneas. The author reserved tomorrow for clinical nutrition: chili and bananas. Bow to smartphones.

Sterilized weapons are reserved for runners with real estate. Integers mourn sad airports, but are pregnant with life. Button up for messy cartoons and reliable cruisers. Let kids live. A football region quivers a lot, but not for long. Ugly laughter is reserved for sterilized freedom. Clinical air conditioning stresses the valley, unless vehicles target the massive chili. Who competes in the relay? Kids with innovative pain pills reserving sad vehicles. The life of sterilized football propaganda. Tomorrow, the element of time will agnostically spark the regional airport, but Oxford will always be free of the EU. The latest outdoor temperature is a throat enveloped by arrows, ugly. An eon curses the veil of fermented time.

Maecenas sodales aliquet ligula hendrerit dapibus. Donec ac nibh sed justo aliquam condimentum eu a risus. Suspendisse fermentum lacinia justo vel imperdiet. Fusce ut nulla nulla. Sed ultricies vulputate neque, hendrerit ultrices eros gravida et.

Vestibulum convallis consectetur congue. In eu tellus nulla. Vestibulum eget velit vitae nibh ullamcorper fringilla. Donec ut leo vitae lacus venenatis sodales. Praesent bibendum convallis risus a mattis. Pellentesque bibendum varius urna, quis tincidunt nisi fermentum eu. Pellentesque cursus interdum tortor, nec vehicula quam fermentum sit amet. Suspendisse potenti. Quisque commodo tristique nisl sed rhoncus. Aliquam faucibus commodo imperdiet. Ut imperdiet laoreet tincidunt. Nunc velit risus, auctor condimentum sodales et, egestas eu orci. Fusce rutrum vehicula metus sit amet commodo. Pellentesque rhoncus, tellus vel rutrum elementum, mi sem porttitor erat, et semper eros orci in mi.

Donec placerat cursus arcu et faucibus. Donec vitae est sed nibh rutrum commodo. Pellentesque elementum pellentesque lectus, in congue magna suscipit et. Nunc sed dui at sapien interdum mattis. Phasellus ac ipsum dui, in lobortis metus. Nunc ligula metus, cursus et porttitor sit amet, interdum eu libero?

Members of Mensa bury protein, but the laughter of dozens of footballs is like an orca until it reserves some banana sauce. A warm hairstyle skirts massage therapy. No, no. However, an utricle's dark gravitas neither winds nor impregnates a basketball. A peanut is a gate.

The main entrance of the valley lies across the country in a region without football. Visit a blue egret veiled in a night life of clamoring alder buckthorn. Unfortunately, as a lion venerates life, laughter is sofaless. In the present real estate market, drink from various urns in order to develop a nutritional football warm-up, but only in the valley. Tempters argue with mace intercut with tartar sauce. Sit inside a mantic vehicle that warms up smartphones. Each convenience is sad for the players, such as the latest orange hairstyle. A convenience in the throat is like a lariat to financial developers. Now remember, the author wants laughter sauce, but your will wants clinical football and clinical make-up. Fear an important advantage, vehicles for kids. Textiles made up of earth's elements are a salad. She was always dear and clinical and liked to ride ferries.

Invest in running until the throat bows. Please live a long life, but also chat with kids who graduate from nutrition by planning for loud elements and making it. Now, sapiens receive DUIs, but sometimes they receive real estate instead. A paella acts like scum in a laboratory, while a meatus seeds a reversed tongue. Fear the now. A lot of ferries run for free, but sometimes a football player needs to bow. Tomato soup is very mainstream, so it constitutes an ecological zero. Resume the pain, itself.

Elit pellentesque porttitor lobortis a graphic designers ut develop usus est placeholder layout de project scriptor visual quin si maxime semantic contentus Hyrcano bello distinebantur. Hoc ducit suam originem ipsum lorem 1.10.32-3 sectiones sunt repetenda est scriptor thesis quod dolor Cicero, De finibus bonorum et malorum (proposita bonorum et malorum). Hic in manuscripto recreat Cicero V-volumen per ipsum lorem Latina, in loco, qui postea fuit translatum ad libro 1-4 1.2.9e QuickLatin usura Google Vertere in quinto libro, bene sequitur spellcheck Affabilitatem Patefacio Muneris et MS Verbum MMVII, secundum conventus Canadian de Anglis. Fons textus huius libri octo est a generantibus buy online placeholder:

www.lipsum.com
www.lorem-ipsum.perbang.dk
www.lorem-ipsum.info
www.ipsum-generator.com
www.blindtextgenerator.com
www.designerstoolbox.com
www.subterrane.com
www.loremipsumtextgenerator.com

THE PROCESS ITSELF

Lorem ipsum is a placeholder used by graphic designers to develop a project's visual layout without being distracted by any particular semantic content. The origins of lorem ipsum have been traced to sections 1.10.32–3 of Cicero's thesis on the existence of pain, De finibus bonorum et malorum (The Purposes of Good and Evil). This manuscript recreates Cicero's 5 volume tome using lorem ipsum in place of Latin, which was then translated into English using QuickLatin 1.2.9e and Google Translate, followed by a thorough spellcheck courtesy of Open Office and MS Word 2007, according to the conventions of Canadian English. The source text for this book originates from eight online placeholder generators:

www.lipsum.com
www.lorem-ipsum.perbang.dk
www.lorem-ipsum.info
www.ipsum-generator.com
www.blindtextgenerator.com
www.designerstoolbox.com
www.subterrane.com
www.loremipsumtextgenerator.com

ADDITAE

Legiones quae erga christum atque confinia filiorum Zimmerman pro numine, et Marcus Timmons ad opinionem, et Jonathan Ball est patientia, et Jason Dewinetz pro consilio, et Rachel Zolf et Craig Dworkin ad meridiem, et Timotheus Kennedy ad ipsum stella, et Laurea Monocotyledones McPherson et pueris meis ad vitam.

Progymnasmata de apparuit tibi in sectiones ex manuscript *Descant, memewar, Tangere Balaam,* et *Facti*Simile,* quod multo impotentiorem subito torcular ut ex a digital chapbook.

ACKNOWLEDGEMENTS

Phalanxes of gratitude to Caleb Zimmerman for the inspiration, to Mathew Timmons for the belief, to Jonathan Ball for the patience, to Jason Dewinetz for the guts, to Rachel Zolf and Craig Dworkin for the glow, to Jake Kennedy for the very star, and to Laurel Eckhoff McPherson & my boys for the life.

Sections of the manuscript have appeared in Descant, memewar, Touch the Donkey, *and* Fact*Simile, *as well as a digital chapbook from ungovernable press.*

www.ingramcontent.com/pod-product-compliance
Lightning Source LLC
LaVergne TN
LVHW101320110826
845152LV00016B/160/J

* 9 7 8 1 9 4 7 3 2 2 0 0 4 *